Sail On

A WOMAN'S
Personal Journey
THROUGH
DEPRESSION

YUXIANG D. ZHANG
TIFFANY J. TOWSLEY

outskirts
press

To my husband, Jason
And to my two children, Wesley and Cassie

Table of Contents

Introduction

It all started in 2012. I was forty-six and fighting pre-meno-pausal depression. The depression lasted for about four months - from late March until mid-July. The days seemed endless as they were shrouded by paranoia, stress, negativity, hopelessness, and grief. I lost my appetite and rarely ate. I lost a significant amount of weight over a short period of time. Overcoming my depression felt like an impossible feat. However with strength and determination I was able to fight and successfully defeat it.

Five years later, my depression has not returned. I will occasionally have an anxiety or panic attack, but I have learned to manage these well. My weight has gradually returned to its pre-menopause state. Sleepless nights have returned to peaceful rests that are only interrupted by an alarm's chimes. I am once again happy, sociable, and more importantly, free. I enthusiastically accept social invitations and indulge in pleasures such as dining out, attending concerts, and traveling abroad.

Thinking back on those days and nights of struggle brought about by my depression still sends chills down my spine.

Nowadays, I have buried all of the negative thoughts deep within my mind where they cannot be easily called forward. Some of my problems still exist, but they do not bother me anymore. My confidence has recovered back to its initial state. The heavy dark clouds have dissipated and my mind is now filled with peace, calmness and clear sunny skies.

As time moves forward, I feel increasingly relieved, lucky, and blessed. I am no longer dictated by the suffering I endured during my depression; instead, I am happy about the outcome. It was through my experience with depression that I truly started understanding it. It's difficult to describe the miserable, frightening, exhausting, and hopeless feelings a person suffering from depression feels. Happiness to the depressed person is like color to a color-blind person. It is inaccurate to think that the depressed are weak or over reactive. Well-wishing statements such as "be happy" or "count your blessings" are of little use to those suffering through depression.

It was during my struggle with depression that I promised myself to share my story with others if I recovered. I would describe my misery, my process of exploring, my remedies, my road to recovery, and my maintenance of a healthy mental state. This book is a manifestation of the promise I made to myself. In this book, I will share my journey through and out of depression. I hope my story will help others suffering through pre-menopausal depression.

CHAPTER 1

What Happened

IT BEGAN IN the spring of 2012, right after spring vacation. In order to catch up with the work that had piled up while I was away, I worked intensively in front of my computer for days. My work is demanding on the brain. It involves writing reports, reviewing data, compiling tables, generating graphs, etc. Within just one or two days, I began to feel down, tired, and irritable.

While having dinner one day, I suddenly felt hot and agitated. I had to leave the table abruptly. From that evening on, I began to lose my appetite. I could no longer taste the food I was eating anymore. I felt agitated to the point where I could not sleep. I began to have frequent panic attacks, often several times a day. Previously, I had only experienced panic attacks about one to two times a year, starting from the age of thirty-five. I was especially prone to attacks while eating and before sleeping. It was during these times that negative thoughts or flashbacks would mount until one would trigger a panic attack. During these attacks, I could not sit, stand, or lie in bed. I gradually lost my appetite to the point where I could not eat or even drink.

When passing by a restaurant, I would look through the windows and wonder how the people inside were able to eat. I wondered if I would ever be able to eat like them, or even like my old self again. At night, I had difficulty falling asleep because of the haunting random thoughts and old memories. If I were to fall asleep, I would usually wake up in the middle of the night and continue to have these thoughts and memories. The memories came back to me in scary images, filling me with regret and guilt. I wanted to look or know things that were impossible to find. My mind became so messy during these sleepless nights that I had to get out of bed several times and pace back and forth in the hallway.

I wanted to escape. I turned down all social invitations. I avoided seeing people. I could not think about social interactions or travel without panic. The fear of an impending panic attack sometimes seemed worse than the attack itself. The scariest feeling was the loss of control during the panic attack and not being able to stop them from coming one after another. Everything I saw, heard, sensed, or thought of could trigger an explosion in my mind. I feared I was losing my sanity. I feared that I was going insane just like the people I saw in movies and read about in books. My confidence level dropped to an all-time low. It was impossible to make decisions without worrying about making irreversible mistakes which might result in regret. I couldn't even click the buy button while online shopping for fear that I would not be able to undo it. Every breath I took was short and shallow. For the first time in my life, I felt like I could begin to understand people who had committed suicide. The misery of depression, constant anxiety, and panic attacks seemed too insurmountable to get over.

About two weeks into my depression, my weight dropped drastically, from 138 to 112 pounds. The sudden weight loss frightened me. I began to worry about dying due to hunger or exhaustion. I knew I needed to do something to rescue myself. The first step I took was to see my Physician, Dr. Y.

Initial Approach

About half a month into my depression, I visited my physician, Dr. Y. I told him that I was depressed. I told him that everything I was surrounded by and everything that came to my mind bothered me. I told him how much weight I had lost, and that I could not sleep. I vividly remember Dr. Y drawing a pie chart divided into five equal pieces which were labeled Music, Exercise, Yoga/Taichi/Meditation, Eat and Antidepressants.

I listened carefully as he explained how each of the five pieces could help me cope with my depression. I took the drawing home to further evaluate each of his suggestions. In addition to following the pie chart, Dr. Y recommended I make an appointment with Dr. S, a Psychologist, for a psychological exam and diagnostic interview.

After Dr. S interviewed me, she told me that she believed I was not suffering from depression. For half an hour, she listened to me explain the things that had been bothering me. She then tried to explain away every example I gave her. I could not blame her for not understanding that my depression was not the result of any one specific thing but everything in my surroundings, inside and out. Tears flowed from my eyes from time to time as I listened and spoke to Dr. S. I wondered why I was so weak. Towards the end of the interview, Dr. S said that she could put me on antidepressants if that's what I wanted.

Antidepressants

I told Dr. S that I was worried about the side effects and addiction associated with antidepressants. I was also worried about the risk of suicidal thoughts that might come about once I stopped using them. Dr. S assured me that the newer medicines were far better than the old ones. They were not addictive and I could safely stop taking them at any time. I told Dr. S that I was not ready for a prescription for antidepressants but that I would contact her if I changed my mind. Out of the five pieces of the chart that Dr. Y gave me, the fifth one, the antidepressant, was eliminated first. Although I wanted an immediate cure for my depression, I believe in natural remedies over taking medicine. I am knowledgeable about drugs and medicine as I've spent my entire career working with them as a chemist in the pharmaceutical industry. All drugs have side effects, especially those which act on the brain. This is why I was very cautious about taking antidepressants. I believe that our creator enclosed the brain in a blood-brain barrier to block most compounds from entering in order to protect the brain from harmful materials. That being said, I also believe in drug discovery and development scientists. These scientists work hard to aid those suffering from depression and anxiety by introducing safe and effective antidepressants. Although I turned down a prescription for antidepressants, I felt comfort in knowing that the option was there as a last resort. After deciding to take antidepressants off the table, I had four other pieces from the pie chart to consider.

Music

I've always loved music whether it was pop or classical, with or without words. Music enhances my mood and relaxes my mind instantly. Before my depression, music brought forward good memories and joy. I loved to sing all the time. However, during my depression, I found all kinds of sounds annoying, including music. Additionally, at times when my mind was particularly fragile, some songs or lyrics would trigger something unpleasant that would induce anxiety or panic attacks. I decided that I needed my surroundings to be as silent as possible, so I took music off the table.

Exercise

During my depression, I tried to exercise every day. At lunchtime, while everyone else was eating, I would walk to a nearby park. Every evening after dinner, I would walk around the neighborhood for one to two hours. I could walk on and on without feeling tired. When I walked, I had the strange feeling that those around me somehow all appeared depressed. After my walks, I would usually stay outside for as long as possible, staring at the dusky sky and watching the birds fly. I often longed to become one of those seemingly free birds. The peace and quiet that nature provided was soothing and drew my attention away from worry. Exercise surely brought a momentary peace of mind. However, even while walking and enjoying nature, my breath was still short and shallow.

Taichi

"Taichi is a bunch of adults, rubbing their tummies, slowly" described my son when he was little. However, it is more than that. Taichi was developed by the ancient Chinese and encompasses the forces of yin and yang as they relate to movement. Through moving, one can control, guard, and re-direct the mind.

I explored Taichi as an option to harmonize my body and mind. During sessions, I attempted to follow the master. I tried to stay focused on my body's movements while keeping my mind from wandering. However, my mind seemed separate from my body and I could not stay focused and control my thoughts. I moved mechanically like a zombie, while my mind was lost in chaos.

After class, I conversed with the master. He told me that the highest level in Taichi was to achieve control of the mind by being able to re-direct thoughts to the ones you want to have.

I asked the master if practicing Taichi could help with sleep-lessness. He said that it could, and that he was able to fall asleep the moment he lied down without even remembering the feeling of his head touching the pillow. I admired his level of mastery, but I realized that this level of mastery in Taichi would be too big of an endeavor for me to achieve.

Eat

Using Google and Baidu, I searched for foods known to make people happy or to balance their yin and yang. I tried following the recommendations my searches provided. However, during my depression, I lost my desire to eat or drink. Even though I found that certain foods could help clear and lighten my mind, my limited food intake interfered with the effectiveness of such a remedy.

Whenever my mind allowed me to, I started exploring other ways to help me return to my previous state. I started reading books, searching online, and talking to close friends and relatives. During that period of time, Google and Baidu were my two best friends. It was reassuring to know that I was not alone in my depression. The stories, tricks, and tips shared by many others served as stepping stones on my quest for peace. I asked question after question and gleaned answers through my studies, extracting practical solutions for myself to put to the test against my own suffering.

What Are Anxiety, Panic Attacks And Depression Like?

In order to move forward, it was important for me to understand depression, panic attacks, and anxiety on an academic level. I called depression, panic attacks, and anxiety my three-limbed monster. This three-limbed monster might have been living inside of me for years and was mostly dormant until recently, when it suddenly sprang to life.

There are various definitions available from different sources. I chose definitions for each limb of my three-limbed monster that fit my situation the most. According to the American Psychiatric Association's definition for depression[1] , "Depression (major depressive disorder) is a common and serious medical illness that negatively affects how you feel the way you think and how you act. Fortunately, it is also treatable. Depression causes feelings of sadness and/or a loss of interest in activities once enjoyed. It can lead to a variety of emotional and physical problems and can decrease a person's ability to function at work and at home." Per the Anxiety and Depression Association of America, "A panic attack[2] is the abrupt onset of intense fear or discomfort that reaches a peak within minutes and includes at least four of the following symptoms: palpitations, pounding heart, or accelerated heart rate, sweating, trembling, or shaking; sensations of shortness of breath or smothering." And, as stated in Wikipedia, "Anxiety[3] disorders are a group of mental disorders characterized by feelings of anxiety and fear. Anxiety is a worry about future events and fear is a reaction to current events. These feelings may cause physical symptoms, such as a fast heart rate and shakiness. There are a number of anxiety disorders: including generalized anxiety disorder, specific phobia, social anxiety disorder, separation anxiety disorder, agoraphobia, panic disorder, and selective mutism. The disorder differs by what results in the symptoms. People often have more than one anxiety disorder."

For me, depression was like a small kick, hitting me constantly throughout the day and night. The accumulation of these hits over time drove the life out of me. Panic attacks were more like big blows or a sharp stab, lasting between a few seconds to minutes. I knew the blow was coming, but I was unable to avoid it. Anxiety was like the fear of an oncoming blow. When would it come? How severe would it be? The frequent anxiety and panic attacks knocked me over and made me feel insane and completely out of control. They could happen at any time in response to any situation, sight, or thought. They were miserable and acute, whereas the depression was more chronic. The latter could last for days or even weeks. While I was suffering from depression, I felt anxiety and had panic attacks three to five times per day.

It is difficult to find words that can truly express the chaotic, muddy, and cloudy scenes that plagued my mind. My mind was broken, unable to function, completely possessed by the three-limbed monster. It was like my mind was overridden by natural disasters. It was like a sky covered by dark clouds. It was like a sailboat in a tempest, at constant risk of tipping over and sinking. It was like the unpredictable nature of a tornado or earthquake. It was like a tsunami, silently gaining power before exploding into destruction. When I was depressed, no one seemed to understand how I felt inside, how heavy my mind was, how much I resented myself. I often cried in silence, trying in vain to use the tears to flush out the three-limbed monster that controlled me.

I've spent my whole life collecting and understanding quantitative measurements, but I could never measure the depth of the chaos going on within my mind. Responsible for proposing trends, I somehow couldn't see my own. How much misery could I sustain? How would I keep it under control? How long would I wait before peace returned?

Night after night, in the silence of the darkness, I was so sleepy, yet I could not sleep. Fear, sadness, and feelings of being trapped with no way out took turns knocking me over. Sometimes, tears flowed without any reason. It might have been the silent cry for help. I was no longer myself. I could not turn my mind off from its auto-link to fear, regret, and dead ends. Many times, I jumped up out of agitation. Sometimes I clenched my teeth, cursing, but it was all in vain. These auto-links continuously flashed, firing on and on. Inevitably, these thoughts intertwined at a dead end and created a huge wave of incomprehensible panic.

This reminded me of Hemingway's book, *The Old Man and the Sea*. In the darkness, lost at sea, and by himself on his little boat, he was overpowered by sharks. He knew they were coming, but there was nothing he could do to stop them. In my case, the sea represents the combination of internal and external factors, housing and surrounding the brain. The power of the sea is so unknown, unmeasurable, unpredictable, uncertain, and yet decisive. Just as the old man could not predict, or prepare for the sharks' attacks, we cannot prepare for the fear panic attacks bring when they hit. We can only wish to fight off the fear when it attacks, just like the old man did with the sharks. Perhaps this theme is what Hemingway had in mind.

I also thought about F. Kafka's book, *Metamorphosis*, where a person suddenly transforms into another form or being, completely coiled within his own world. His story seems so bizarre and untrue. Was this a manifestation of the author's situation? To some extent, this is exactly how a person going through depression might feel or behave. He or she may retreat into his or her own world without caring about or being understood by the outside world.

These two books combined represent what I was going through. Sanity is like a sailboat. Most of the time we sail along through calm seas. There are sometimes bumpy waves to overcome, but overall we navigate just fine through life. However, in stormy seas, a sailboat, just like our sanity, will most likely topple over and bob up and down uncontrollably. No matter how loudly we yell for it, our sanity may be lost to the turmoil of the waves, rocks, and wind. Only when the storm subsides, can the sailboat recover and return to sailing freely upon the open waters.

Stubborn Negative Thoughts

According to Wikipedia, "an intrusive thought is an unwelcome involuntary thought, image, or unpleasant idea that may become an obsession is upsetting or distressing, and can feel difficult to manage or eliminate". I tend to think that negative thoughts are sourced from our day to day lives. They are part of what makes us unique and sets us apart from other animals.

Like animals, one of the primary purposes of humans is to produce offspring. To fulfill this purpose, we need to eat, drink, and stay safe. When we are born, we seem as simple as animals. We eat and play. As we grow older, we learn. Society begins to place expectations on us. Humans are more complex than animals because animals have no such applied expectations or pressure to find purpose in life.

Every day we compare and compete amongst ourselves. Poor people want to be rich. Rich people want to be richer. People in power want more power. At work, we are separated by levels of power: managers, directors, vice presidents, presidents, CEOs. CEOs for small companies want to become CEOs for large companies. There are always bigger, better carrots dangling in front of us, keeping us in an endless chase.

Each one of us is a subordinate to someone else. We have to behave in certain ways and meet expectations. We are constantly judged and reviewed for status, salary raises, and promotions. For some, coping with the unavoidable chase for more and pressure to meet expectations, becomes the only purpose in life. The real purpose in life becomes obscured.

When ones' purpose is not clearly defined or seen, vanity, greed, and jealousy may arise. In addition to the burden of negative thoughts resulting from such traits, we have responsibilities and tasks to complete. We also have ordeals and the fear of separation or loss of our loved ones. Modern communication magnifies the adversity of others and makes it all too easy to believe that all of the terrible things happening to people could happen to you, to your family, and to others you know or care for. Little by little these scenarios are brought upon us. We carry on, but the stresses and fears accumulate and bury themselves inside our mind. Eventually this pressure must be released, as tension is released during an earthquake. So a second aspect of life which sets us apart from animals is the negative thoughts resulting from our daily struggles and fears.

That being said, isn't it true that the negative thoughts are always on our minds? I had negative thoughts prior to my depression but was able to cope. I would sometime feel melancholy, but overall my mental state seemed fine. Why was I now unable to cope? What changed? Interestingly, negative thoughts are not equal in and out of depression. In our normal state, we can identify where the negative thoughts are coming from. We can reason and ease negative thoughts away. Sanity is intact and prevents us from diving deeper into our negative thoughts. However, the negative thoughts brought on by the three-limbed monster are baseless, ridiculous, and without logic. The three-limbed monster diminishes our level of sanity and in turn, our ability to control our negative thoughts and respond to them.

Negative thoughts alone did not cause my depression. It was my diminished ability to control them and my responses to them at the moment. My sanity was not well enough intact to stop, re-focus, or re-direct the cascade of negative thinking. Even when nothing was happening, my brain somehow managed to search for and accumulate any hint of negativity in the outside or inner world. It was me who lost the capacity to handle, revaluate, accept, and channel the negativity out. Was this due to the physiological and chemical conditions within my body? When everything lines up just so, does it induce the perfect storm? Does it call forward the three-limbed monster? If so, does our mind have a reset button?

The question of whether I could reset my mind gave me a tangible, visible, and controllable resolution. My hope was that searching for and finding the answer would help me restore the normal condition of my brain, body, and mind and bring back the original, happier me. With this goal in mind, I started to pay less attention to the thoughts of self-pity, resentment, and bad luck. I tried to focus less on crying over simple things, and more on the question of "now what?" The first step for me was learning about the brain, body, and mind.

How Does Our Brain and Body Work Together?

To gain a better understanding of how the brain and body work together, I began reading books on them. After digesting many books, I came to my own definitions for the relationships between the brain and body.

Our body activities consist of the following three parts:

- Hardware - the brain and the body.
- Software - the commands, emotions, logical thinking, reasoning, memory, point of view, etc.
- Action - physical activity, carried out by the body consciously or unconsciously.

The software directs our body to act in certain ways and not in others. The hardware, our brain, hosts our mind. There are two theories on how the brain passes signals (i.e. how nerve cells communicate). It is said that the brain passes signals by soups or sparks. One is a chemical process involving the release of chemicals. The other is a physical process involving electrical communication. Nerve cells, or neurons, can send an impulse to another neuron through the synapse, which is the tiny gap across nerve cells. The transmissions of signals across a synapse are carried out by chemical messengers, known as neurotransmitters. The mind works through synapses firing, which controls certain functions of the body.

Our software, the mind, handles our emotions and thoughts. The mind co-exists with the brain and body as software co-exists with hardware. Usually the mind tells the body what to do. I wondered if easing the body could ease the mind. I wondered if the brain's discomfort could affect the mind and the body. With these questions in mind, I decided to try the approach of soothing my mind by comforting my body.

Could this three-limbed monster of mine be the result of things I did or did not do? Was I overworked, or was I suffering from a chemical imbalance? These inquiries kept me actively looking for answers and most importantly seeking solutions.

In The End, I Survived

Apart from my quest for answers and solutions, my family was the main reason for me to fight against my depression and survive. My husband would sometimes walk with me after dinner. He silently listened to me with the occasional nod of approval. When I got to the point of telling him that I felt like a total failure not deserving of his love, he would patiently list out all of the things he thought I was amazingly successful at. His encouragement eased my mind a little, but it was not enough to scoop me out of the state I was in. My kids started being quiet around me. My state of mind swept away the lighthearted conversations, jokes, and laughter from everyone, silencing the entire house. One night, I was meditating on the floor in a closed room with the lights off. My daughter, without knowing I was there, came in, saw me, and retreated, closing the door quietly. Later on, my husband told me that she started crying. I was not able to care much. This made me feel even more agitated with guilt and helplessness.

Between panic attacks, when I was able to think normally, I thought about my kids' suffering. It gave me the strength and desire to fight. My family was the main reason for my recovery. The preservation of my family awakened my defense mechanisms. I was determined to no longer allow each visit from the three-limbed monster take me over. I decided to face it. I had to live.

I started carefully paying attention to my mental state, logging my panic attacks and practicing tips and tricks for dealing with the chaos in my mind. I extracted the factors under my control and explored each of them in hopes that I could find a way to cope. After each panic attack, regardless of its intensity scale, I would observe myself and collect data. I would collect all of the data I could. Some aspects seemed subtle and trivial. However, I wrote them all down. I was collecting raw data - the more the merrier. Of course I would prefer to not go through any episodes, but if one would come up, I would start thinking about my diary and get a little excited about entering the good raw data that might come of it.

I examined all of the data I collected. I tried connecting dots, looking for patterns, establishing connections, and finding the cause. I tried singling out certain factors over other factors. I searched google to find similarities and reinforce cause-and-affect relationships. I used the data I was collecting as well as my analysis of it to come up with hypotheses for the cause of my depression, anxiety, and panic attacks.

I would test my hypotheses then come up with more data. I rejoiced whenever I confirmed a hypothesis and collected data that affirmed my techniques. Through trial and error, I discovered that thinking of myself as a guinea pig seemed to help me. The other approach was dealing with my depression, anxiety, and panic attacks like a puzzle I had to solve, like an escape room. According to Wikipedia, an escape room is "is a subgenre of point-and-click adventure games which requires a player to escape from imprisonment by exploiting their surroundings." During a panic attack I would try to imagine I was locked up in the prison and would try to escape. I acted as a player looking for clues and figured out how to escape the current situation and return to the normal world. When my defense or escape mechanism kicked in, I was amazed at the inner strength and intelligence I possessed - the will power, the persistence, the sharpness, the self-control, the power of a warrior to pursue peace and happiness for myself and for my family.

I would also use music to inspire me to keep fighting. To boost my courage in escaping mode I would silently sing "Hero" by Mariah Carrie to awaken my courage.

> "...And then a hero comes along
> With the strength to carry on
> And you cast your fears aside
> And you know you can survive
> So when you feel like hope is gone
> Look inside you and be strong
> And you'll finally see the truth
> That a hero lies in you"

I would sing it whenever I recovered my sanity for a little while, to gather up some strength. I would do this for a few seconds before the next wave with my hands clenched in a fist and teeth ground together. When possible, I would pick up my pen and notebook, write my observations down in a diary, and sharpen my weapons against depression a little more. Like a fighter, I would escape from the anxiety and panic attacks and return to peace. The breakthroughs in my studies and my escape quickly made me smile.

The battle involved several phases. Phase I (myself, the guinea pig) was to understand myself as an experimental subject. Phase II, understanding my background, characteristics and traits, will be described in Chapter 2. Chapter 3 is the pivotal section of this book, as it links back to the promise I made to myself five years ago; the promise that I would share my story with the hope of helping others. In Chapter 3, I describe my approach to healing based on modern science and Chinese medicine. It is my hope in writing this book, that people in need can apply the solutions described in Chapter 3 to themselves and pass through the darkest era of their lives to become happy and content once again. In Chapter 4, I will share my strategies for coping with anxiety and depression in detail, and explain how I dealt with each situation. Chapter 5 will focus on maintaining a healthy mental state and some continuing after thoughts.

For now, my three-limbed monster may be asleep or trapped inside a cage. My depression is mostly gone and I am able to control my anxiety by using my tips and tricks. I still experience panic attacks from time to time when conditions present themselves. However, I am happy to say that the frequency of my panic attacks has returned to my pre-depression rate. I hope you can use this book to help yourself and others in the fight against the three-limbed monster and to sail on peacefully in life.

CHAPTER **2**

All About Me

INITIALLY DURING MY depression, I was totally lost and overwhelmed. I was constantly questioning myself. Some of these questions included:

1. I don't have anything to complain about in my life. Why am I so depressed?

2. Each woman goes through menopause, but not all of them go through depression. What is so unique about me? Where does my tendency to be attacked by the 3-limbed monster come from?

3. Am I mentally ill? If so, why now?

4. Am I ever going to recover? Is this misery going to end?

5. Is taking antidepressants going to be my only option for fighting the 3-limbed monster?

6. I have known people who have committed suicide. Will I suffer the same fate?

7. If each experience has its own meaning, what is the meaning of this depression for me?

8. What is the purpose for me living on anyway?

I considered myself as the subject in my own psychological research study. In studying myself, I collected first-hand information: information about my own characteristics, which I hoped could provide clues about how I became depressed, and eventually could lead me to a resolution.

My Upbringing

I came from a big family of five siblings. My father was a retired military pilot. He first served in the Korean War around 1953. Later he became a military pilot. He flew the turboprop airliner TU-102 and turbojet-powered airliner TU-104. The TU-104 was the first jetliner that China bought from the Soviet Union. At the peak of his military career, he decided to return to his home: a small village in the outskirts of Beijing. There, he worked as a farmer for the rest of his life.

My mother never attended school. She was a full-time housewife who mostly stayed home to take care of the family. She was my hero and my North Star. She always inspired me to do the best in school. When I started to learn how to read, she would open my Chinese book and ask me to recite the words and stories which she never had the opportunity to learn. She always paid full attention to my stammers. Even though she didn't read, she came up with her own unique way to help me learn.

However, we had our difficult moments. Our lowest point came when she burned my books and notebooks. One night while trying to study, I complained to my mother about my younger sister being too noisy. My attitude set her off and she threw my books and notebooks into the fire and chased me out of the house into the darkness. I ran as far away from her as I could to avoid being beaten. Growing up, one of my greatest fears was the darkness. However, in this moment, the darkness was not as intimidating as my mother's fierceness. I was more frightened by this situation than I was about the ghosts in the night that might jump out at me. I ran directly to my best friend's house and stayed the night there. The following day, everything else seemed to revert back to normal except me. I decided to skip school because I wanted to avoid the embarrassment and shame of my situation. In addition, I didn't have any books. I wandered around the whole village all day. I longed to go back to school because the lack of schoolmates to play with made the village incredibly quiet and boring.

Two or three days later, from my hiding spot, I saw the school principle and my classroom teacher visit my house after dinner. I made sure that they saw me but stayed far enough away so that they could not grab me and force me to go inside. After a few minutes, my mother came out with them. I was right at the entrance now, eavesdropping. Once they finished conversing, my mother escorted the principal and classroom teacher out through the entrance. As they passed me, they smiled at me and instructed me to go inside. I saw my mother smiling during the entire conversation and the smile did not go away when she saw me. Seeing her smile assured me that it was safe to go inside the house. When I got inside the house, she hugged me. I cried over her warmth and forgiveness. I learned then that, for better or worse, I needed to control my temper or suffer the consequences.

My mother would often described beautiful images of city life, where women dressed nicely, rode horses with wavy hair, and ate delicious food. She told me I could achieve this type of life only through my own effort. This unseen picture accompanied me throughout my entire childhood. I worked hard by listening to teachers and actively taking part in the classroom problem solving sessions. Because of my competitive nature, I was always at the top of my class in math and Chinese. These were the only two subjects in elementary school at that time, and my classmates trailed far behind me. All of my teachers liked me and gave me extra, more challenging work to do.

In 1978, two years after the end of the infamous Cultural Revolution, I graduated from elementary school. That same year, China changed its education system dramatically. The school started to organize classes based on student performance. The top one hundred kids in my county were selected to attend a boarding school funded by the government. I felt fortunate to be among the one hundred kids selected to attend one of the top three boarding middle schools, with classes taught by some of the most dedicated and knowledgeable teachers. This was a turning point in my life.

My Education and Career

After middle and high school, I took the college qualifying exams. These qualifying exams are intense and competitive. Students are given one opportunity to take the exam, the results of which will most likely determine their future. Because my middle school was among the best, a few students each year would qualify for the best colleges. Despite the fact that most students were not even able to qualify for a college education, I felt blessed to be able to attend one of the top schools in Beijing for a BS degree in Chemistry.

I graduated from college in 1987 at the age of twenty-one. At that time, the government would assign jobs to all graduates. I was given a list of job openings to choose from, so I chose to work at a food testing laboratory. My first job was to measure sugar content in grape samples gathered from the field. I never knew there were so many different types of grapes! We used titration, a common analytical testing method, to determine sugar content in the grapes. Titration involves the chemical processes of reduction and oxidation. One sugar molecule, the reducing agent, will consume one molecule of the oxidizing agent. Oxidant is added to the grape juice until the end point of the reaction is achieved – when all of the reducing agent has been consumed. The percentage of sugar within the grapes can be determined using the volume of oxidant added and a simple calculation. After each test, I would go ahead and eat the left over grapes. With my sugar content results at hand, I knew which ones to pick. After a while, my tongue became so educated that I was able to guess how much sugar content a grape had just by tasting it. My tongue could determine the amount of sugar within one percent of the measured value! I enjoyed my first job very much. Being able to determine the unknown using science was very satisfying for me.

In 1992, after working for about four years, I decided to

advance my education in the land of hope and opportunity, the United States. I earned a Master's degree in Organometallic Chemistry from Syracuse University and, soon after, landed a job as a chemist at a nutraceuticals company. The company manufactured garlic power for use in garlic tablet dietary supplements. My job was to determine the allicin content in each batch of garlic power produced. Allicin is a chemical believed to have health benefits such as lowering cholesterol and triglycerides. It is also believed to have an antidiabetic effect.

After two years working in nutraceuticals, I got a job at a pharmaceuticals company. I have been working in the pharmaceuticals industry since then and have helped develop a variety of drugs, such as human growth hormone (rhGH), antidepressant, antipsychotic, sleeping pill, acute pain killer, cancer, HIV, AIDS, and Hepatitis C drug, among others. My first project was to test a drug called DITROPAN XL. It was an extended-release tablet containing drugs that treat urinary incontinence. The drug was designed as a once-daily controlled-release tablet to be taken orally. My job was to test the tablets to ensure that more than ninety-percent of drug released into the body in the period of 24 hours. Therefore, the amount of residual drug left in the tablets could not be more than ten-percent. My next job was at a company which focused on rapid delivery of the drug to the patient. These drugs could be delivered into the patient within a few minutes and were used for sleeping disorders, panic attacks, acute pain, and schizophrenia. These drugs were designed to be inhaled into the lungs for fast delivery into the circulatory system. Clinics were excited about having such fast acting inhalable drugs for people with schizophrenia since they would keep staff from having to use needles when chasing patients.

For the past ten years, I have been working as an analytical scientist in new drug discovery and development. My work has been in product stability. For every bottle of medicine, the label states the dosage (i.e. 200mg), storage condition, and shelf life (i.e. store in cool place for 24 months) of the drug. My work supports the validity of this label. At regular intervals for the 24-month duration, the lab tests the appearance, assay, degradation product, water content and dissolution of the drug. At each specified time interval I need to test the tablets to ensure that the labeled dosage (i.e. 200mg) is indeed the amount of drug in the tablets, that there are no impurities generated that are harmful to the human body, and that the tablet disintegrates and releases the drug into the digestive system within the required time.

Recently, the company I work for acquired a new and revolutionary cell therapy for fighting cancer called CAR-T. This new therapy can prolong the lives of terminally ill cancer patients by months. Even a few days of prolonged life may allow a patient to be able to see their children's graduation or wedding day. I feel that I am contributing to a body of work that can potentially make a huge difference in peoples' lives. Even though my contribution to drug development may be very small, I enjoy my job. I have learned to be critical and agile. Through my work, I have developed strong problem solving skills. I am content in my career and feel a sense of accomplishment in helping people.

Overall, my journey in life has been smooth. I feel as if I have been given more than I deserve. Together with my husband's income, we are a middle class family and own our home near Silicon Valley outright. We have enough income for our kids' education and family travels. Our two kids are hardworking and are doing well in school. My son studies Chemistry and my daughter studies Computer Science and dreams of working for Pixar someday. I count my blessings all the time and feel like something more powerful than nature is watching over me and giving me the best.

My Physical Characteristics

I was an athlete when I was young - a sprinter. I could not run well for more than 400 meters. My body was not genetically equipped to supply enough energy to carry my muscles through long, intensive activity. I am more suited for explosive movements. This may have something to do with the high level of adrenaline in my blood at the time.

I have tiny veins. Drawing blood from me is always a challenge. The technician has to poke me many times before hitting my vein. I have to lie down and squeeze my hand many times for my veins to come forward. Because of my tiny veins, my blood circulation is not very strong. My job requires me to sit in front of the computer for eight hours a day. This sedentary behavior does not help my circulation. I also have the habit of crossing my legs while sitting which also interferes with my circulation. Poor circulation may result in less nutrition and oxygen flowing to each part of my body. Metabolic waste may be removed from my body more slowly than in others with better circulation.

I have fast reflexes. It seems that my brain doesn't take much time to react when spotting danger. My fight-or-flight response is strong.

I am not very coordinated. I believe that my cerebellum may be smaller than others'. In humans, the cerebellum plays an important role in motor control, and it may also be involved in some cognitive functions such as attention and language as well as regulating fear and pleasure responses. I often play poker and always admire those who can make the cards fly from one hand to the other so flawlessly and skillfully as they shuffle. When I was younger, I tried to learn how to do the same. I practiced hard, but my shuffling never improved. In sports, I was only good in sprinting. I was not able to do anything that required heavy coordination like the high-low bar or swimming.

My Genetic Characteristics

One of the first thoughts I had when I decided to study my own depression was to look at my family history. I traced my mother's family history for depression and found no one. However, my great aunt from my father's side committed suicide. She threw herself into a pond and drowned. I was about ten years old when it happened. It was a November day and the water had just started to freeze. This was the first time my mom and I ever talked about death. After my great aunt's funeral, I kept asking my mother questions. I wanted to know why my great aunt jumped into the water when it was so cold. I wanted to know why her husband, my great uncle, did not hear her get up, get dressed and leave the house. I wanted to know how she found her way to the pond in the middle of the night and if she was afraid.

My mother was a superstitious person. She believed in the Yin space and the Yang space. The Yin space is the place where people live after death. The Yang space is for the living. She said that a ghost called my great aunt in the middle of the night, so she followed the voice into the pond. This frightened me very much. As an adult now, I believe that my great aunt's suicide was most likely the result of depression. I did some quick math and figured that I share one eighth of my genes with my great aunt. My genetic makeup could make me more prone to depression as well.

My blood type is B. My two best female friends also have blood type B. It is believed that B is the blood type of artistic people, meaning that they have impulses of emotion, love change, and hate routine as it lacks excitement. It is a colorful and passionate blood type. My husband is blood type O. It is believed that O is the blood type of leaders. They have strong willpower and are fascinated by blood type B's carefree, instantaneous nature. As my blood type may make me a more passionate person, I get easily frustrated when I am rejected or blocked. When I am rejected or blocked for something I want, I usually find a way to get it. However, I quietly keep the frustration hidden inside of me.

My Mental Characteristics

I have Claustrophobia. I did not realize this until I was thirty-five years old. My first experience with claustrophobia occurred one day after eating lunch inside my office. My office was a long, narrow room with two desks. My co-workers sat at the desk closest to the door. All of the sudden, while sitting at my desk, my heart started pounding, and sweat poured from my forehead. The agitation I felt was so overwhelming that I had to stand up and go outside the building immediately. I had to circle around for a while before I started to settle down. The feeling I experienced subsided after a few minutes.

I went to my physician to talk about my attack. He said that I might have claustrophobia and that I could leave any room at any time if I started to feel the same way. He said that, if I needed medicine, he could prescribe Prozac. This shocked me because I thought that Prozac was an antidepressant. My physician informed me that claustrophobia and panic attacks are treated with antidepressants as well. I was worried that having claustrophobia made me an insane person. I couldn't think of any reason for me to have claustrophobia - I could not recall any trauma and I had never been locked up in any small spaces. After my first experience with claustrophobia, I noticed that even thinking about being in small spaces, like being in an MRI machine, made me feel uneasy and panicky.

I had postpartum suicidal thoughts. I would not call what I experienced after having my second child postpartum depression. I did not have symptoms, like sadness, reduced energy, anxiety, changes in sleeping or eating patterns, crying episodes, or irritability. However, I did experience suicidal thoughts on two occasions. I recall having lunch with a friend and, while still sitting at the dining table, I had this random thought of killing myself. In that moment, all of my surroundings went dim. After a few seconds, the thought disappeared. Fighting back my feelings of shame, I asked my friend if she had ever experienced the same thing. She had just given birth to a baby two weeks ahead of me. She nodded her head and said that she felt it sometimes too. She brushed it off like it was no big deal and said it was pretty normal for women after delivering babies.

The second time suicide came to mind, I did not treat it like a big deal. The thought went away without me realizing it. I was busy living my life of work, commuting, paying the mortgage, and taking care of two young kids, a new born and a two-year old. I recall that, at that time, I believed I had no reason to hate my life. Nothing was bothering me and my days were normal. If I had known that depression would find me years later, I would have kept a diary to record all of the details in my life occurring prior to my brief suicidal thoughts. I would have recorded what I ate, when I went to sleep, how many times I was awakened by crying babies, which exercises I did, how my work load was, if I drank enough water, if I ate too much sugar or not enough sugar. The first time I had a suicidal thought was during a meal. It seems like my stomach and my mind work together. During my pre-menopausal depression, I had no appetite. My mind did not want me to put anything into my stomach. For me, the avoidance of eating or drinking is an indicator of a mental problem. Knowing what I know now, the connection between my stomach and my mind has always been there for me to uncover.

I don't drink, I don't smoke, and I've never done drugs. I am a clean freak in terms of putting things into my body. I feel like drugs and alcohols negatively affect my body's normal chemical composition and environment. I don't even take cold medicine unless I absolutely need it. I am always more attracted to nature's remedies as a first line of defense. Again, I believe that the blood-brain barrier has a reason to exist. Some molecules like those in nicotine, marijuana, heroin, and alcohol are able to pass through the blood-brain barrier. I called these evil compounds. These evil compounds make people high, excited, and feel good. However, they impair normal function. I don't want any of these materials to sneak inside my brain. However, during depression, the brain itself is messed up and needs help. To bring it back to normal, I was open to experimenting with antidepressants for a period of time.

I am naturally timid. I believe that I inherited this temperament from my grandmother, who passed away when my mother was seventeen years old. My mother told me that my grandmother had died from fear – that she had been scared to death.

When New China was born, the peasants were liberated by the liberation army. In the New China, these peasants, the proletariat, who were previously exploited, became the master class. The peasants were now in power and control and some of the rich were put on trial. People from the whole village would gather to watch these trials play out. The richest people of the village, the land owners, were humiliated in front of the crowds. They were publicly beaten to release the hatred that the poor had harbored for the rich. It was punishment for the rich's exploitation of the poor.

One night, after returning from a public trial, my grandmother became frightened by the sounds of people beaten wailing like ghosts in the dark. She became frightened that her family would eventually be put on trial as well. Her family was comparatively richer than most of the other farmers in the village. She was so frightened that night, that the fear never left her.

She was bedridden after that night and died shortly thereafter. My mother said that my grandmother's bile-producing organ may not have been functioning correctly. The Chinese say that when a person dies of fear, it is because their gallbladder burst as a result of the intense fear.

I remember that I was afraid of going out in public when I was young. My mother tried to train me to be brave. She would ask me to go buy groceries for her, but I would often refuse to go. She would entice me to go by giving me one extra penny to buy candy for myself. I would take the money and move my feet slowly along the side of the small street to avoid people's eyes, hoping that there were no customers in the store. When I got to the store, I would stand behind people with my head down not daring to say a word. One of the clerks knew me well and usually came out from the counter to help me. He would hold me up over the crowd and ask me to point at what I needed to buy. In this way, I was able to get all of my mother's groceries, plus one candy, without saying much. Afterward, I would go home quickly to see my mother's satisfied face. To this day, the smell of the grocery store always pleases me as it reminds me about the kind-hearted clerk and the times he held me out over the crowd.

Fear is associated with the hormones epinephrine or adrenaline.[4] Abnormally high adrenaline levels are positively correlated with a person's tendency toward negative feelings and fear. I believe that I may produce higher than normal levels of adrenaline. It may be that my adrenaline regulating system does not function well. Adrenaline may also help the conversion of fear into memory. It is no wonder that I can recall scary scenes so vividly. The feelings of fear are etched into my memory by the action of adrenaline.[5] My physiological response to fear might be encoded in my genes.

I am afraid of public speaking. Prior to any of my talks or presentations, my mouth becomes dry and my heart starts pumping rapidly. I have difficulty concentrating and I feel disoriented. The most embarrassing moment in my life happened while I was giving a speech at the age of about seven or eight years old.

The speech was outside on the playground in front of the whole school. I remember feeling so anxious and afraid. My teacher had written the speech and wanted me to read it. The speech had a few new words in it that I had never learned the pronunciation for. I practiced these new words the night before, but during the speech, I became so nervous that I forgot the how to say them. I started to turn red from embarrassment and skipped the 1st new word, then the 2nd, then the 3rd, until finally, I started to cry. My tear drops fell onto the paper and smeared the rest of the words on the page so that I was no longer able to read the rest of the speech at all. I stood there not knowing what to do. Then, a strong gust of wind blew my papers away. I ran after them and, after many deliberate attempts, was able to stomp my foot on the papers, preventing them from continuing to fly in the wind. I forgot what happened afterwards. I probably just went back to be with my classmates. To this day, I still remember the immense embarrassment I felt.

I am afraid of snakes. Just looking at a snake can set me off. When I was about twenty-one years old, a friend took me to the Beijing Zoo to show off his knowledge of animals and plants. When we got to the reptile exhibition, I insisted on staying outside, but he dragged me in. I took my glasses off before going in so that I wouldn't be able to see anything clearly. The stealthy coiled snakes imagined gave me chill through the whole exhibition. Since then, I've had multiple encounters with snakes while camping and hiking. Despite these moments happening many years ago, my memories of these encounters are so vivid. The fear I experienced is stored deep within in my mind. My husband loves snakes. He is much braver and calmer than I am. Maybe people who are afraid of snakes are more prone to being timid and sensitive like me.

I am very sensitive and observant. I always watch peoples' faces and worry about whether they are happy with me or not. If someone has an angry face, I wonder if they are mad at me about something I may or may not have done. I have a tendency to point everything back at myself and look for explanations for everything happening around me.

I tend to be very emotional. My feelings can be overwhelming and can take control of me. During these times, logic and reason are completely abandoned. I lose arguments with my husband because when my emotions take over, I cannot back myself up. My husband, however, can stay cool and provide stories and examples to support his points and draw out the flaws in mine. I only win arguments when I cry and make him feel guilty. My tears are always my best weapon against my husband when we argue.

I hold grudges against people who have humiliated me. In my life, there are people who I have never forgiven and others who I've been able to forgive completely. It all depends on my mood. Maybe this has something to do with my adrenaline levels at the time the humiliation occurred.

I don't like being judged. We are judged all the time - especially in work during year-end reviews. Every day throughout the year we are judged in small bites, and are then devoured at the end of the year during our review. I always feel uncomfortable during this time. Looking back on my career, the only time I felt free of this type of judgment was when I was a consultant. I felt so happy and free. I was free to leave work without feeling guilty, free to work anytime I felt like it, and free to take long vacations without worrying about losing my job. However, consulting did not provide the same practical benefits as full-time permanent employment such as paid vacation, sick leave, subsidized healthcare, and reduced taxes. For these practical benefits, I sacrificed my freedom from judgement. However, the good memories from my time as a consultant are always shimmering in the back of my mind.

I am impatient. I have a short attention span and a bad temper. Some people have the ability to discuss a controversial topic or make an argument patiently, slowly, and gracefully, but I do not. If I compare these styles, it's like others are playing ping-pong and I am playing basketball. Whenever my husband and I argue we both reach our highest pitch and intensity within five minutes. We then turn away from each other and go into different rooms to avoid seeing one another. The silent treatment can last ten times longer than the argument itself. The waiting always frustrates me since I prefer an instant resolution. In life, we must wait for many things. The impatience and frustration accumulate and get stored within.

My Childhood Dream

When I was young, I dreamt of becoming a doctor. I naturally want to help when I see people suffering. However, when I was seventeen years old, my grandfather died of a stroke and I changed my mind. A few years earlier, I had promised to cure his illness. When he died, I was devastated and felt like I had lost my purpose. Even though I never became a doctor, helping people through their suffering gives me pleasure and a sense of accomplishment. The smile I can bring to people by helping them always brightens up my day.

Things that Make Me Happy

I love music. Music is my number one source of entertainment and serves as my escape. Listening to the words and melodies brings me tears of happiness and joy. It can be my best and most loyal friend during emotional times. I love pop music, music with or without words, and classical music. Bette Midler's songs always touch my soul. I love the song "Wind Beneath my Wings." I feel so blessed to have so many people in my life to lift me up - my parents, my siblings, my husband, my kids, teachers, mentors, co-workers, and friends.

When I have a big chunk of time to myself, I listen to classical music by Tchaikovsky, Mozart, Beethoven, Chopin, Bach, Debussy, and other similar composers. When listening to this music, I immediately retreat into my own world. These masterpieces must be the result of God resonating inside the minds of the geniuses who brought them into this world. On the power of song, I believe that Franz Kafka said it best in his short story, "Josephine the Singer".[6]

[When a singer is singing] The real mass of the people—this is plain to see—are quite withdrawn into themselves. Here in the brief intervals between their struggles our people dream, it is as if the limbs of each were loosened, as if the harried individual once in a while could relax and stretch himself at ease in the great, warm bed of the community... Something of our poor brief childhood is in it, something of lost happiness that can never be found again, but also something of active daily life, of its small gaieties, unaccountable and yet springing up and not to be obliterated...[music] set free from the fetters of daily life and it sets us free too for a little while.

I love flowers. The world of music is like a thousand flower gardens filling my soul with joy. Flowers have the ability to instantly cheer me up. Some flowers have fragrance, while others do not. Some have vibrant colors, and some are dull. Some cover the ground, and others climb. Some bloom in the spring, and others in the winter. Some open in the morning sun, and others open up at sunset. Some react when touched. Some love water, others love dry conditions. Some bear flowers all year long and others bear flowers for only one day. The perfect symmetry of flowers and combinations of colors always amaze me. Being in nature, even if only for a few minutes, calms me down. I am easily cheered up by flowers and music.

My Religion

My mother believed in Karma, and this was the philosophy I was brought up in: the actions of each person determine his

37

or her destiny in the next incarnation. This philosophy made me feel like I was being watched, resulting in my own hidden self-judgment that always ran in the back of my mind, constantly building pressure. The other Buddhist philosophy I was brought up in was the idea that life is full of suffering. I was taught that all people are here in this life to pay for their sins from their last life. The people who are not in this life have made it to live eternally in heaven. The goal in this life is to do enough good to pay off the debt accrued in past lives. Only the best will be able to escape the Karmic cycle and live eternally in heaven.

All of the hurtful things I had done growing up remained in the background of my life. I often feared how I would be judged in the afterlife and worried about whether or not I would be punished in my next life. These fears and worries drove me to Christianity. In Christianity, the Almighty power would forgive the bad things I had done if I asked for forgiveness. All of the wrong-doing, whether intentional or unintentional, could be cancelled out. This idea removed the regret, self-guilt, self-hatred, pain, and fear I had been experiencing previously. I could be saved and go directly to heaven.

I envied people who had faith in God. I saw real joy on the faces of people who believed that the Almighty was accountable for the unexplained, so I attended a local church for Bible study. However, the more I studied, the more questions I asked. I brought my kids to church with me as well, and they had questions of their own. One day, my daughter asked me the following with puzzled eyes, "If God created people, who created God?" My little daughter was thinking just like her mom. I bit my tongue to hold back the answer I wanted to give and said instead that God exists like how the universe does: that neither needed creation. Author Richard Wright wrote, "the meaning of religion, the hunger of the human heart for that which is not and can never be, the thirst of the human spirit to conquer and transcend the implacable limitations of human life."[7] His thoughts on the human spirit resonated with me.

I continued to go to church until one morning when the priest said that the biggest sinners in God's eyes were the non-believers. This statement made me feel uneasy as I had my own doubts on God's existence. I decided to stay away from church in hopes that God wouldn't notice me until I became a true believer. Years passed, but this topic of whether God considered my doubtfulness as sin still existed in my mind. Over time, my husband and I agreed that we could neither prove nor disprove the existence of God. During my depression, I went back to church because I thought it would help me. However, I wasn't able to stay. I felt that gaining peace through worshipping God would not be quick enough to quench my immediate thirst.

My Point of View – The Relationship between Me and the World

I think of family as a living cell. Society is like a living organism consisting of family cells. When each cell is healthy and functioning well, the whole society works well. The sea pen is a good example of this. According to the Monterey Bay Aquarium Sea Pen exhibit:

A sea pen resembles a plump, old-fashioned quill. Each tiny animal in a sea pen colony has a mouth and eight feathery tentacles. Groups of these animals work together. Some feed and others pump water. If annoyed, the whole colony acts as one.

Every time I go to the Monterey Bay Aquarium, located at Cannery Row, Monterey, California, I stand in front of the sea pen aquarium for a little while and admire them for the fascinating and puzzling way they organize, divide work, and function together. Sea pens live in colonies. Each individual executes its duties of digesting and cleaning. As a colony, they survive well and avoid being eaten by predators. In human society, each family member is an individual sea pen. In order for the colony or society to function well, each family needs to be well. If there are threats to each individual's well-being, the whole of society should be relied on for defense.

As a parent, I may not be perfect. I usually create heat between myself and my kids when I am educating them and sharing my life lessons. My intent in educating them is to shine light on the right paths so that they may become productive members of society. I am confident that my kids won't go hungry or fail in life, but I wonder if they could achieve more had I created more light and less heat in bringing them up.

Within society there are experts in each field who are passionate about the work they are doing. Their findings shine light on their subjects of study. With so much knowledge in society we see more in the world and are able to help each other. Like Confucius said, "when I walk along with two others, from at least one I will be able to learn." We are all interdependent. When in trouble, we should rely on each other and society. The whole society serves as the wind beneath our wings. We can draw from all of the knowledge and experiences of others to find remedies to our own problems and reach our own goals towards happiness.

My Best Trait

I have come as far as I have in life because of my curiosity and problem solving skills. At work, problems must be solved accurately and efficiently. When confronted with a problem, I will typically look at all of the procedures and data available and then compile a summary. I then investigate deeper by looking at other related information and discussing the problem with others. I evaluate all of the information collected, sifting through non-critical factors and looking for patterns and relationships. My evaluation usually results in hypotheses to work from. Most of the time, I lead myself in the right direction towards the cause and solution of the problem.

I am not a type of person who beats around the bush. For me, solving problems is as easy for me as writing a poem is for a great poet. I take great pride in my work. After solving a problem, I always smile to myself with satisfaction. The truth is a beautiful thing. With the application of hard work, the right skill set, and a sharp intuition, any problem can be explained or solved.

CHAPTER **3**

My Remedies and Routines for Coping with Depression

THE FOLLOWING REMEDIES and routines helped free me of my 3-limbed monster. These personal techniques are listed in order of effectiveness and include explanations on how they came to me and why they worked. They did not come to me easily and orderly; rather, as described in the previous chapters, they came to me after countless times of independent studying and experimenting.

Early on, I realized that using antidepressants would be my last resort in defeating my 3-limbed monster. I also realized that my brain had been hijacked by hormonal changes from pre-menopause. The hormonal changes–in combination with my genetic background and personal characteristics–potentially made me more prone to depression than others. When the brain is hijacked by depression, the mind becomes almost unusable. Knowing that I wouldn't be able to defeat the 3-limbed monster with my mind alone, I centered around studying my body. Luckily, we don't need a clear mind to be able to move our bodies. During physical activity, the mind may fade into the background, go dormant, or rest.

Squats

Whenever my mind became numb, cloudy, or stuck, I would do squats. I would pay very close attention to my head, specifically the top left region, and continued doing squats until it cleared up. I also did squats whenever I felt an impending anxiety or panic attack. During panic attacks, I would lose sensation in my body. I would not notice the cold air when getting out of bed or the dryness of my mouth and throat. After doing squats, sensation would return to my body and my short, shallow breaths would return to deeper, normal breaths. Doing squats was effective in helping me sleep after waking up in the middle of the night.

When doing squats, I would keep my body straight, squat down with my arms stretched out in front of me, and then stand straight up. I would do about thirty squats per round. At about twenty squats, my legs would start to feel sore, my breathing would quicken, and my pulse would beat more rapidly. After one round, I would take a short break to catch my breath and let my arms and legs relax. Then I would do more rounds until I started feeling my mind clear and my anxiety dissipate.

The following passage from my diary describes one of the many instances where squatting helped me sleep after waking up in the middle of the night:

I woke up after having a bad dream. I couldn't remember what the dream was about, but it caused me to wake up, anxious. It was two o'clock in the morning and I couldn't get back to sleep, so I sat up in bed. This caused my husband to wake up to check on me. Making my husband wake up made me feel guilty and even more agitated. I got out of bed and left the room to look outside. It was a peaceful night. The stars and city lights seemed so lonely – like me. I started walking up and down the hallway to ease my mind, but it was no use. All of a sudden, I remembered that I should try squatting instead. I started with thirty squats, then did fifty. Then I did ten pushups, drank a lot of water, and proceeded to mop the floor on my hands and knees. Around four o'clock in the morning, I felt completely calmed down and decided to sneak back upstairs to bed. I was able to fall back asleep and didn't wake up until my alarm went off! Doing squats worked!

After realizing that doing squats could help me fend off anxiety and return to sleep, I became filled with joy. It was such a fast and easy activity that could be done anywhere.

On one occasion–when I was doing a facial–doing squats saved me from having a panic attack. The room where facials were done was a small storage room with no windows. I was usually fine when visiting the salon. However, during this particular visit, the moment I entered the room, my breathing became shallow and shortened and my anxiety level started to rise quickly. I noticed that my panic attacks often occurred after sitting, lying down, or entering a small room.

The esthetician asked if I was okay. I told her that I was not and asked her to step out of the room. Once the esthetician left the room, I began a series of very quick squats. After about two minutes, the esthetician returned to check on me. By the time she returned, I felt a lot better and was able to lie back down for the whole facial session. I was so happy and relieved to have found such an effective and convenient remedy for my panic attacks!

So how on earth did I come up with such a remedy? It was an accidental discovery comprised of my cross-cultural experiences, past memories, open mindedness, curious nature, and willingness to help others. Before realizing that doing squats could help me, I would often clean the floors on my hands and knees during many of my sleepless nights. On one occasion, I stood up too quickly and became dizzy. In order to lessen this dizziness, my mother suggested that I raise my legs one after the other upon standing up. As I was doing this exercise, I noticed immediately that the cloudiness inside my brain dissipated. At that moment, my mind became clear and I recalled an experience I had twenty years before when I was In Beijing.

I was helping a co-worker take her eight-year-old son to see a doctor who claimed he could cure near-sightedness. The boy had been to this doctor before, so he knew what to expect. I watched as the doctor tested the boy's eyesight and recorded the boy's measurements. He then proceeded to place several small, black, pea-sized solids into his ear. The doctor massaged each solid into several different areas within the boy's ear, and then he secured each piece with tape. After that, the doctor commanded us to start doing squats. I tried hard not to expose my disproval for the doctor's methods in front of my co-worker's son. After a few rounds of fifty squats, the doctor checked the boy's eyes again. To my astonishment, the boy's eyesight had reached 20/20.

I was in my early twenties and I hated wearing glasses. Seeing what the doctor did for my co-worker's son, I asked him to treat me as well. He affixed several pieces of black solids within my ears and asked me to do about two hundred squats per day. After two days, I didn't see my eyesight improving. Out of curiosity, I took the black solids out and broke them open with a hammer. I previously thought that the black solids were made of medicine but was dismayed to find out they were just peas. I threw the black peas away and stopped doing squats. The treatment didn't work for me. However, my co-worker's son continued it and did not need glasses for several years thereafter.

That sleepless night, after having the flash back, I thought more about why the treatment seemed to have worked. I thought about how close the eyes are to the brain. Doing squats seemed to help the boy's eyesight, so maybe it may have also helped the brain clear up. The little boy's story and my mother's trick to reduce dizziness helped me connect the dots.

After discovering this trick, I tried to come up with an explanation. First, I did some reading in an attempt to understand the nervous system during panic attacks I discovered Walter Bradford Cannon's "fight-or-flight" response. Our ancestors developed this fight-or-flight response as a result of having to fight off wild animals to survive. Today, we seldom face the threat of predatory animals. However, our defense mechanisms have been passed down across generations in the form of panic attacks. Panic attacks are believed to be our natural response to impending danger - seen, sensed or imagined. When danger is imminent, there are several physiological processes that involuntarily occur within us to prepare our body to either fight the threat off or run away from it. The nervous system responsible for this response is the called sympathetic nervous system (SNS)[8] which acts on the body parts, causing them to respond by releasing adrenaline and cortisol into the blood stream. The whole body reacts. The heart begins to pump faster, blood pressure and sugar levels increase, and muscles are readied to respond. The counter part of the SNS, called the parasympathetic nervous system (PSNS), is now deactivated. The main function of PSNS is to "rest and digest". As a result, we unconsciously cannot relax or digest food during a fight-or-flight response. At this time, all relaxation techniques like deep breaths, Taichi, and meditation are far-fetched and unachievable since the PSNS functions unconsciously. This may explain why people tend to lose their appetite when they are depressed. Only when we believe the threat is gone will the PSNS be reactivated and the SNS system deactivates. How do we help our body adjust to the SNS-PSNS alternation? With intense muscle movement, we consume energy–the necessary step to complete the natural stress response cycle. By exercising intensely, we trick our body into thinking that the threat is no longer there. When the threat stimulus is no longer there, adrenaline and cortisol levels decrease. The SNS system retreats and the PSNS system re-activates. Doing squats is a perfect activity since squats can be intense and fast. Moreover, physical movement is governed by the somatic nervous system which we can consciously control. I believe that doing squats is my button to reset my body before or during a panic attack.

Some of us are more sensitive to perceived threats than others and therefore respond more strongly. Genetics play a part in how an individual responds to stress. Perhaps this is why certain individuals may be more negatively impacted by stressful situations.

Learning that elevated levels of adrenaline and cortisol are in our blood stream before going to sleep made me realize why my anxiety and panic attacks often occurred at night. Throughout the day our stress levels accumulate. Towards the end of the day, our adrenaline and cortisol levels may reach maximum concentration. If the buildup of fight or flight energy isn't released, anxiety or panic attacks may occur. This may explain why I would often experience heightened anxiety or panic attacks when lying down. Lying down in a relaxed state does not consume as much energy as moving. Sustained levels of adrenaline may provoke negative thoughts and bring forth bad memories etched into our mind.

I've noticed that shortening of breath is an indicator of "fight-or-flight." I would suggest against going to bed unless you can breathe effortlessly. This can be achieved through intense physical movement. Doing squats forces the thighs to work vigorously, increasing blood circulation throughout the body and most importantly, to the brain. Each squat forcibly squeezes the large artery in the thigh, thus speeding up the flow of blood to various parts of the body. The increased blood circulation quickly supplies the brain with oxygen and nutrients necessary to strengthen normal functions. Metabolic waste is simultaneously cycled out of the brain more efficiently. The act of doing squats helps return the brain and body to a more balanced state, and, in turn, eases the mind and stops panic attacks in their tracks. In my mother's words, "a fast heart beat will drive away the demons that fear hot red blood and the sound of a beating heart."

Hot Water Foot Baths

Another helpful remedy in easing my anxiety was the simple action of soaking my feet in hot water for about twenty minutes. If the water cools before twenty minutes is up, hot water may be added to keep the temperature up. To help ease my anxiety, I would do this before going to bed every night.

I learned about this remedy from my parents. In 2001, my mother-in-law became gravely ill. Our relatives informed us that we should travel back to China as soon as possible to say our goodbyes. We spent two days on planes and trains to get there only to learn that she had passed away while we were on route. I remember my husband falling to his knees, sobbing with sadness and guilt for not being there for his mother's last moments. For several days afterward, we made arrangements for the funeral. We were all exhausted. To make matters worse, I was worried about my son. Before we left for China, he had tubing inserted Into his ears to drain the fluid accumulated during his reoccurring flu. We stayed in my husband's hometown for about a week. After the funeral, my husband decided to stay with his father a little longer. I decided to take the kids and fly back to Beijing to see my parents.

I spent the first night at home in Beijing chatting with family members. The following day I started feeling agitated. I could not sleep, and the sounds of people talking and the TV really bothered me. The hot weather and bright lights also started pestering me. Everything that came to mind became a nuisance. I was miserable and worried that I was going crazy. Thinking back, my rising anxiety level was most likely due to all the stress associated with the death of our family member: the jetlag, the traveling, the hurrying, and the worrying. All of these things must have added up together, causing my adrenaline and cortisol levels to peak and aggravate my mental state. It was not the heat, the light, the sounds, or the talking that bothered me - it was my nerves getting overworked.

My mother took me to the local hospital to check my anxiety. The doctor who saw me could find nothing wrong and suggested that my anxiety was due to too many things happening at once. He treated me with oxygen for about fifteen minutes and then sent me home. My father had an oxygen tank at home, so it was convenient for me to treat myself with oxygen. While using the oxygen, my parents suggested that I also try soaking my feet in hot water. For about two or three days in a row, I soaked my feet before going to bed. After the third day, my anxiety levels dropped back to normal – as if nothing had happened. I was able to enjoy time with my family for the remaining days. When I started searching for remedies to help my pre-menopausal depression, I remembered how hot water foot baths helped me cope with my mother-in-law's death. I found that it helped ease the anxiety I suffered during my depression just as it had in 2001.

I believe that soaking my feet in hot water helped relieve my anxiety and sleep better because hot water soothes the nerves and speeds up circulation. Sometimes I found it difficult to remain still for more than twenty minutes. In these cases, I would stop soaking and walk around. I would try and soak for as long as I could though, and I was usually able to complete the entire twenty minutes.

Acupressure and Acupuncture

By searching online, I was able to find articles introducing the best acupressure points for anxiety relief. The articles often provided instructions on how to locate each point. I usually used my middle finger to glide over the area where the point was supposed to be located. The point should be more hollow and softer than the surrounding area. When you press down onto the point, you should feel sore. The point is usually pea-sized or the size of the tip of the thumb.

Some people prefer acupuncture as opposed to acupressure. In acupuncture, doctors use long needles instead of fingers. For my own purposes, I would use my own fingers to stimulate my pressure points. I would often do acupressure on myself while soaking my feet in hot water. I would usually spend about two minutes repeatedly and releasing each of the following points:

1) San Yin Jiao (SP 6) – Three Yin Intersection. SP 6 is located on the inside of the leg about three inches into the calf from where the round bone of the ankle (medial malleolus) and foot meet. This point eases the spleen, liver, and kidney.

2) Shen Men (HT 7) – The Spirit Gate. HT 7 is located at

the ulnar end of the distal wrist crease with the palm facing upward. This point calms the mind and eases anxiety and panic attacks.

3) Nei Kuan (PC 6) – The Inner Pass. PC 6 is located in the inner forearm area about two inches from the palm between the two bones in the lower arm. This point reduces insomnia.

There are many acupressure points to help increase appetite, cope with menopause, calm nerves, and improve other general emotional disturbances. It is up to the individual to discover which points work well for his or her own condition. Its healing process as takes longer then pharmaceuticals, so patience and faith are important when using acupressure. However, the method has been proven to be effective and has been practiced for over two thousand years. I hear testimonials all the time from people who have benefited from acupressure. My personal story with acupressure began in elementary school.

One afternoon–while I was walking around the village–I saw a small group crowded around a moaning woman. A doctor was on the ground helping her. The doctor inserted a needle into the woman's leg and as he turned it, the woman gave out a small cry. After a few minutes, the doctor removed the needle. The woman immediately stood up with a smile on her face and claimed that she had felt much better.

It is to my understanding that acupressure points serve as passages and between the outside of the body and inner organs or nervous system. Stimulating these points should have a soothing effect on specific organs. Though there is no empirical or pathological evidence of acupressure's existence, I theorize that there are unseen channels within the body. Think of a person struck by lightning. The electric current from the lightning bolt passes through the body from its entry point to into the ground. This channeling may indicate that there may be passages throughout the body, invisible to the naked eye. Acupressure points leading to specific organs do exist.

Based on others benefitting from acupressure and acupuncture along with my faith in the ancient Chinese practice, I tried acupressure on myself as a way of relieving my depression. As I mentioned before, the results may be gradual, but the method is worth trying. I believed acupressure was a benefit to me, even though it wasn't instant. I hope that acupressure and acupuncture effectiveness can be proven by science. Acupressure appealed to me as a non-pharmaceutical option for easing my depression. It was easy to do and brought no harm in my quest of defeating my 3-limbed monster.

Meditation

To combat my depression, I would often meditate before going to bed. I would begin with five deep breaths and would then sit down with my feet pressed together and my hands covering my feet. I would keep quiet and try to feel my body. About half way into my meditation, I would start to feel the blood pulsing into the palm of my hands. My palms would become moist and warm. One day, I wrote in my diary that "after I felt the blood pulsing into my hands, I started to smell a fragrance, like a flower. It made me feel happy. Later on, I realized that the fragrance was from the freshly washed comforter I was sitting on. I realized this afterwards, but it still made me happy." The diary entry shows that my senses became heightened by meditating

I would also meditate first thing in the morning. If I woke up without a clear mind, I would usually stay in bed. I would put another pillow beneath my head, place one hand on the back of my head, and place the other hand on top of the first hand. I would lie this way for about five to ten minutes. This allowed me to feel the condition of my mind, calm down, and gather the strength to get up. I believe in meditation as a daily practice for recalling the beauty of life, counting the blessings, and training the mind to focus on positive aspects.

Sleep

Sleeping is vital for regular brain functions. The relationship between my sleepless nights and the 3-limbed monster was like the chicken-and-the-egg scenario. Was my lack of sleep causing the chaos in the mind, or was the depression and anxiety making it difficult for me to fall and stay asleep? I never quite figured it out. I tend to believe that the lack of sleep causes depression and anxiety. Practically speaking, it doesn't matter which causes which. It is well known that to lead a happy life, one needs enough sleep. This doesn't only apply to people suffering from depression. Any sleep-deprived person will become short tempered, easily irritable, and impatient.

Influenced by my mother, I've found myself wondering if the lack of sleep allowed for negative energy to be absorbed in the middle of the night when the Yin elements were supposed to be active. In ancient Chinese medicine, it is believed that during each segment of the night, a specific organ is detoxified. Falling asleep before eleven o'clock is necessary to ensure that there is time for the cleansing of organs and the resetting of nerves. I am not sure if this is true, but that's what I was taught.

Our bodies run on an internal clock. We rise and fall with the sun. Our body temperature and cortisol levels fluctuate depending on the time of day. In the morning, body temperature is lower. Cortisol levels naturally tend to be higher in the morning than in the evening. Having high Cortisol levels in the evening may interfere with a good night's sleep since Cortisol increases heart rate and prepares muscles for action. Not getting enough sleep may affect the body's critical regenerative activities. Few sleepless nights are fine, but chronic insomnia will affect the brain's normal cycles and mental functioning.

During my depression, I read books and talked with friends and relatives to learn natural ways to help me sleep. I found that the following tricks worked best for me.

- Expose your body to sunlight. Sun exposure has been linked to increased production of Serotonin. Serotonin converts to melatonin at night. Melatonin is a hormone that aids in sleep.
- Don't overeat
- Soak your feet in hot water for twenty minutes every night before bed. Soaking your feet in hot water improves blood circulation which increases the transport

of oxygen and nutrients throughout the body and brain while removing waste.

- Place pressure at the San Yin Jiao pressure point (SP 6), for about two minutes before going to bed. Refer to Chapter 3 on how to locate the SP 6 pressure point. The He Gu pressure point (LI 4), the Shen Men pressure point (HT 7), and the Nei Guan pressure point (PC 6) are also very helpful. Details on each of these pressure points can be found by doing a quick Google search.

- Don't go to bed when your breathing is short and shallow. For me, doing some type of vigorous exercise helps get me breathing deeper. Doing about thirty squats works best for me, but pushups or sit ups are also effective in getting me breathing deeper.

- Don't go to bed with an unsettled mind. Read, play Sudoku, or watch TV to distract and ease your mind.

- If darkness triggers a scary thought and image, leave a light on.

- Make yourself as comfortable as you can when you get into bed. Arrange your bedding so that when you become sleepy enough, you can fall asleep peacefully without moving or adjusting anything to get comfortable.

- If you wake up in the middle of the night and can't fall back asleep, get out of bed and do some sort of physical activity. Clean the floor, tidy up the house, do squats or pushups, etc. Make sure to drink plenty of warm water to relax and make sure you are hydrated. Do not go back to bed until your mind is clear and calm.

Eat a Balanced Diet

In order to live, we need to eat. However, when catastrophes or tragedies happen, we may avoid eating. Our mind and emotions can affect our appetite. We either deprioritize eating or the system sending messages from the stomach to the brain becomes inactive. Whether our appetite is intact or not, we need to eat and maintain a balance diet.

Our bodies and our brains require all sorts of nutrients to function properly. We need fuel to produce chemicals and hormones involved in neurotransmission. Most hormones or steroids are biosynthesized from starting materials like amino acids or cholesterol. I learned that eating nutritious foods like bananas, whole grains, oatmeal, and other fruits made me happy. I also started taking a Chinese herbal supplement that was recommended to me by a friend. It was a supplement of assorted grains, seeds, and roots called Qing Liang Bu, which translates to clear, cool supplement. The exact ingredients can be purchased at Chinese grocery stores and are as follows: pearl barley, lotus seeds, dried dioscorea, dried lily bulb, fox nuts, dried longan, and dried polygonatum.

The mix was supposed to reduce the Yang in foods that were meant to be Yin according to the Yin-Yang food chart.

I used the herbal supplement in a porridge that I would split into several small portions and keep in the refrigerator. I would have one bowl of the porridge every morning. I faithfully followed a balanced diet and took the herbal supplement for weeks until my depression was gone. Soaking my feet in hot water and massaging acupressure points also helped when my depression kept me from eating properly. I'm not sure if my diet and supplements had a direct impact on ending my depression. However, I did ask my step-mother-in-law to try the herbal supplement, and she commented that her body felt clearer after she drank the porridge.

Keep a Diary

After experiencing severe anxiety or a panic attack, try recalling and writing down anything and everything that could have contributed to it. Try to document what you ate, what your emotions and mental activities were like, and what you did the day or night before. It is also important to document the same things for the days where your mental state improved. In my experience, writing things down in the middle of a panic attack was too overwhelming. However, collecting information after an attack is very useful in finding causes and trying to prevent repeated occurrences.

The diary is your collection of raw data. You can find connections and narrow down possible causes for the anxiety or panic attack. Raw data can Include weather, workload, food and drink intake, physical activities, emotions, experiences, and the quality and quantity of sleep. Collecting enough data to uncover connections and causes can be a lengthy process, so being diligent about writing in your diary is important. With this task in mind, each panic attack can turn into an opportunity to gather more data to use in fighting the 3-limbed monster.

Use Knowledge to Empower Yourself

Many scientists have dedicated their careers to understanding the role of the nervous system, hormones, and chemicals in brain maintenance. Many have studied the causes of mental disease and disorders. These scientists are giants. I stood on the shoulders of these giants, using their work to help me understand my own depression. Below is a summary of the research I did. I am not an expert in these fields, so this summary may seem surfaced. However, the following content seems to explain my experience and observations.

Dopamine and Serotonin

There are two important pathways within our nervous system which affect our behavior, mood, memory, sleep, and pleasure. These pathways are the dopamine and serotonin pathways. Dopamine pathways, also known as dopaminergic projections, are comprised of projection neurons that synthesize and release dopamine. This group of pathways is involved in many functions such as learning, reward systems, motivation, and neuroendocrine control. Serotonin pathways are comprised of projection neurons that synthesize and release serotonin. Serotonergic pathways innervate areas of the brain involved in functions like eating, emotional processing, and mood.

Each pathway is comprised of a series of neurons connected to each other through synapses. Synapses are voids between neurons where neurotransmitters act. Neurotransmitters are like little boats which pass messages from one neuron to the

59

next, completing emotions, feelings, or thought processes. Dopamine and serotonin are small monoamine neurotransmitters which greatly affect the normal functions of our mind. Dopamine is involved with desire, addiction, and the pursuit of pleasure. Serotonin regulates mood, keeps us from going awry, and helps ease anxiety. A lack of serotonin in the brain is thought to be a cause of depression.

By studying these neurotransmitters, we can understand the mechanisms for antidepressants, sleeping disorders, and anti-anxiety drugs.

Dopamine, Adrenaline and Cortisol

Dopamine[9] is a small chemical with one amine group (-NH2). The structure for dopamine is shown below:

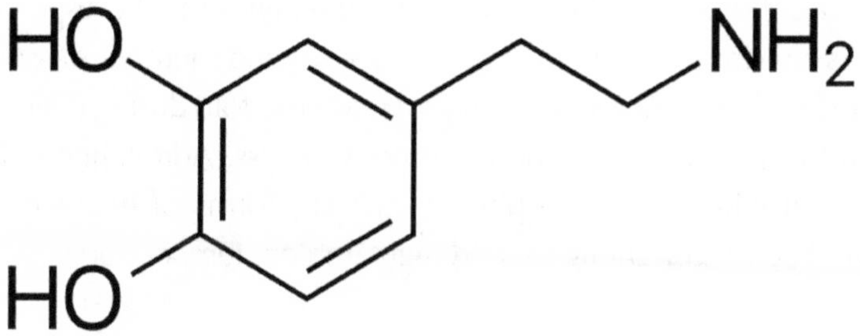

Dopamine

Adrenaline[10] is derived from dopamine. The structure for adrenaline is shown below:

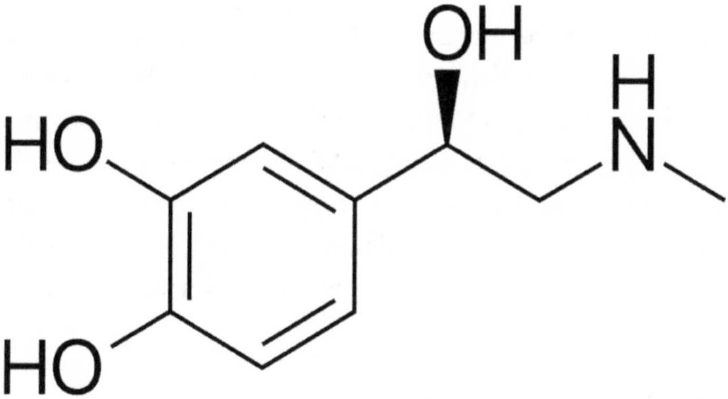

Adrenalin

As shown in the structural diagrams above, dopamine and adrenaline are very similar. Both have a benzene ring bearing two alcohol (-OH) groups. Adrenaline is also known as epinephrine

61

and is the chemical responsible for the fight-or-flight response. It is also involved in emotional responses and memories associated with fear. Adrenaline may increase ten-fold during exercise and fifty-fold or more during times of stress. Adrenaline is released when there are physical threats, forms of excitement, loud noises, bright lights, and high ambient temperatures.

Another chemical that is released in response to stress is cortisol.[11] Cortisol is biosynthesized from cholesterol within the body. Cortisol can be lifesaving in times of danger as it maintains fluid balance and blood pressure, while temporarily suppressing non-critical functions - reproductive drive, immunity, digestion and growth. Cortisol is reduced in times of relaxation and happiness. Lack of sleep, caffeine, stress, and traumatic situations increase cortisol levels.

Dopamine, adrenaline, and cortisol excite and set us in motion in times of stress or danger. High levels of these chemicals make it hard for our bodies to shut down. Low levels of these chemicals may make us feel empty. Maintaining balanced levels of these three chemicals is vital to achieving a healthy mental state. There are several natural remedies that can decrease these chemical levels, all of which can be found by searching Google.

Serotonin and Melatonin

I refer to serotonin as a happy angel from Heaven. It is responsible for maintaining mood, behavior, appetite, sleep, memories, and the sex drive. Serotonin makes us happy. There is a link between the lack of serotonin and depression.[12]

As shown in the following structural diagram, serotonin is

biosynthesized from the amino acid L-Tryptophan,[13] one of the twenty-two natural amino acids that are supplied from our diet.

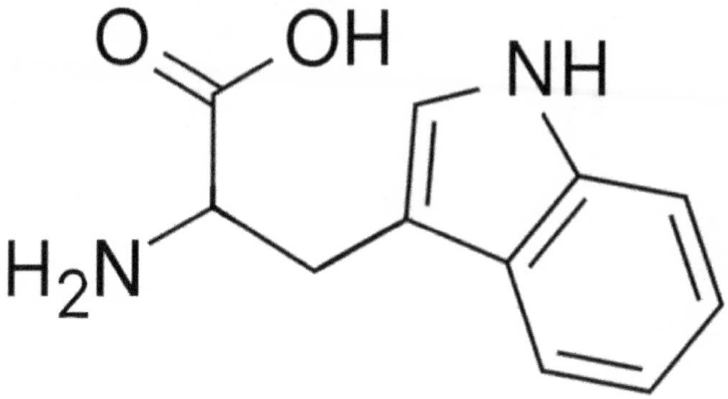

Tryptophan >

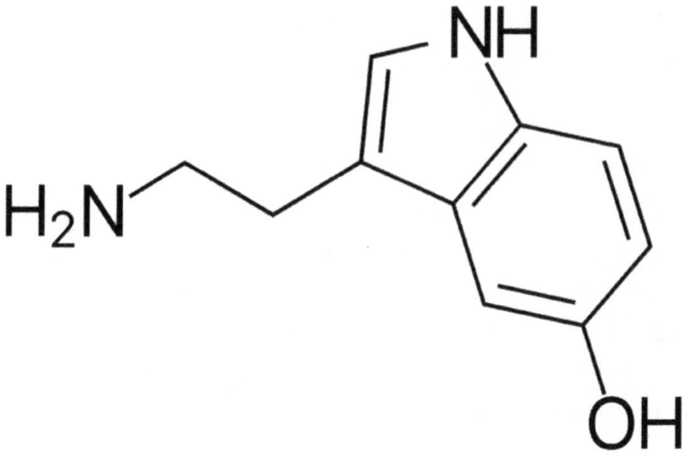

Serotonin >

Melatonin

Serotonin reacts in the presence of enzymes and is con-verted to melatonin[14]–the well-known hormone associated with sleep. Isn't it interesting to know that the chemicals associated with happiness and sleep are so closely related? There are several natural ways to increase serotonin levels. Melatonin can be purchased as a supplement to treat jet lag and insomnia.

Estrogen and Progesterone

During pre-menopause and menopause, our hormones change. As we enter menopause, our sexual functions fade as we produce less estrogen and progesterone. Just as we stopped producing growth hormones at a certain age, our bodies stop producing sexual hormones at a certain age. This is decided by nature.

Researchers have found that estrogen is not only involved in regulating female reproductive functions but in serotonin production as well.[15] Progesterone, on the other hand, seems to reduce the level of serotonin in the brain. During the pre-menopausal years, estrogen and progesterone levels begin to fluctuate. The imbalance of these hormones, along with serotonin, affects our mood. This may be the root cause of pre-menopausal depression. The state is a longer, more un-predictable, and intense version of pre-menstrual syndrome (PMS).

Sex hormone levels fluctuate for a few years during pre-meno-pause and then decline at menopause. After menopause, the body stops producing progesterone. When this happens, es-trogen is the main sex hormone in play, and mood improves. I recall my older sister and my step-mother-in-law telling me that they felt happiest post-menopause. Five years after my pre-menopausal depression and menopause, I believe that I feel the same as they did. I feel calmer, more understanding, more sympathetic, more tolerant, and more appreciative of everything in my life. I am less competitive now and get along with people well. The positive mental and emotional state I currently enjoy may be attributed to the work of estrogen and serotonin within my body.

A Note on Anti-psychotics and Antidepressants

Although I did not take antidepressants in my fight against the 3-limbed monster, I recall feeling comfort in knowing they were available in case I really needed them.

Anti-psychotic drugs, such as Alprazolam (Xanax), act on do-pamine. This class of drugs is designed to block or restore the action of dopamine on the brain to slow the nervous system down. Anti-depressants act on serotonin. There are two categories for antidepressants: selective serotonin reuptake inhibitors (SSRIs) and monoamine oxidase inhibitors (MAOIs). SSRIs prevent the re-absorption of serotonin, thus keeping serotonin levels high and elevating our mood. Common examples of SSRIs are fluoxetine (Prozac), citalopram (Celexa), and sertraline (Zoloft). Some recreational drugs, such as cocaine, work in a similar fashion as SSRIs. MAOIs block the action of an enzyme called monoamine oxidase (MAO). MAO is involved in the breakdown of serotonin. By inactivating MAO, MAOIs increase the concentration of serotonin throughout the nervous system. The MAOIs are used less often than SSRIs. An example of an MAOI is isocarboxazid (Marplan).

By understanding the mechanisms of anti-psychotics and antidepressants, I became less frightened of having to potentially use them. They act with the purpose of restoring the chemical balance between dopamine and serotonin, the devil and the happy angel. For people suffering through depression, using anti-psychotics and antidepressants for restoration should be seriously considered if its use is recommended by their physician.

CHAPTER **4**

Special Cases

Migraines

DURING MY DEPRESSION I didn't suffer from constant migraines, but I had them often enough so that I couldn't ignore them. Before a migraine, I observed a halo of flashing light that didn't disappear even when I closed my eyes. Within fifteen to twenty minutes of it appearing, a full on migraine would arrive. The halo was like the lighting in a pain storm. A friend of mine once told me that acupressure could relieve the pain of a migraine. I often doubted the efficacy of acupressure, but since my friend had told me that it worked for her, I decided to try. If I also thought that because acupressure acts on the nervous system and that migraines also involved the nervous system, it was worth a try.

The pressure point is located on the hand within the webbed area between the thumb and index finger. Press firmly along the area until you find the most painful spot. Maintain firm pressure on this spot until the pain lessens. One day, I observed the halo coming on and knew a migraine was imminent. I immediately found the pressure point on my hand and pressed firmly. To my astonishment, the halo disappeared within five minutes and the migraine never came. I use this pressure point each time I see the halo forming and it seems to prevent a full-on migraine every time. I shared this tip with my sister who suffers from migraines, and it worked for her too. The pressure point seems to only work in cases where the precursor halo is present. The presence of the halo represents the onset of the pain. Using the pressure point may be able to nip the migraine in the bud, but it may not be as effective once the migraine has started.

Lack of Appetite

I had no appetite when I was depressed. It was very difficult for me to eat or drink. During this time, I couldn't stop thinking that the water in my glass was contaminated with air-borne germs or particles. I was worried that they would infest my body. This type of irrational fear stayed with me all the time.

I didn't want to die of hunger or dehydration, so I needed ways to get around my irrational fears. To stay hydrated, I would prepare several cups of different drinks: plain water, my favorite tea, and soy milk. I thought that drinking from straws was cleaner for some reason, so I put straws in all of my drinks. I would place all three drinks on my desk within arm's reach. Keeping my mind on the computer and my work, I would pick up a cup and bring it to my mouth. Without thought, I would drink the liquid.

Finding food that was appetizing was very difficult. After

trial and error, I found something that was neat, clean looking, and tasty: Wheat Thin crackers. My taste buds enjoyed
the particular texture and flavor of these crackers. I survived
on Wheat Thins for a few weeks. When my appetite slowly
recovered, I would consume foods in small portions like
Chinese Dim Sum. Because I couldn't stand noisy environ-
ments, I would order out and find a quiet place in the park
to eat by myself. I would watch the birds fly and look at
flowers or new leaves on the trees. Nature brought peace to
my mind and distracted me from avoiding my food. Little by
little, I was able to eat more food. After about three months,
I could eat a whole roll at a Japanese restaurant. At first, I
felt uneasy. I thought the music was too loud and started
feeling anxious. I was about to stand up and leave just as the
waitress came to take my order. I ordered my favorite sushi
and ate half of it. Once I started eating, I paid no attention to
the music at all. As I finished, I felt a huge boost in my self-
confidence. Before that meal, I had felt as though I would
never be able to regain my appetite and eat at a restaurant
ever again.

My experience with dealing with my lack of appetite taught
me that we can feed the body through different methods. High
levels of cortisol—due to stress—result in lack of appetite. As
mentioned in Chapter 3, cortisol is part of our fight-or-flight
response to stress. Increasing levels of cortisol increases heart
rate and muscle tension. Eating and drinking is part of our rest
and digestive state. The rest and digestive state becomes suppressed when cortisol levels are high to divert energy to the
heart and muscles in response to perceived immediate danger. Even when the rest and digestive state is suppressed, the
body is still able to function. If we are able to trick ourselves

into eating or drinking, our body will still be able to digest, even if it seems difficult.

Travel

Between work and family vacations, I often need to travel across various time zones. On many occasions, I have felt intense anxiety while waiting for an airplane. On one such occasion, I was travelling with my co-worker. My co-worker had arranged the flights for our trip before I could tell him that I needed an aisle seat. When we boarded the plane, I realized that I was in the middle seat and he was by the window. The moment I sat down between my co-worker and the man in the aisle seat, I felt a current shoot up from my lower back to my head; it felt so hot and stuffy. I had to get up abruptly and stand in the aisle as the people who were still boarding squeezed by. I asked the man in the aisle seat if he would switch with me, but he shook his head no. After a few minutes of standing in the aisle, I calmed down enough to get back into my seat. Stuck between the two men, I was still feeling hot, so I took off my outer clothes, and pulled my hair to the top of my head so that the heat could escape from my neck. The man in the aisle seat must have realized that something was really bothering me because he offered to switch seats with me after all. What a gentleman! I was a lot more comfortable in the aisle seat and felt fine for the rest of the flight.

By studying myself, I learned some things that helped me travel without incident. The following are my suggestions to help reduce or eliminate anxiety while travelling:

- Give yourself plenty of time to pack. Don't wait until the last minute.
- Get plenty of sleep the night before travelling.
- Carry water and stay hydrated. After the security check, buy a bottle of cold water to drink or to splash on your neck and forehead in case you feel hot while sitting down. Being able to cool down is calming.
- Dress in layers to help regulate your body temperature.
- Wear loose, comfortable pants. Tight clothes can be aggravating.
- Always sit in the aisle seat. When booking your flight, make sure to reserve an aisle seat so that you don't need to worry about it right before the flight. In cases where you're not able to reserve an aisle seat ahead of time, ask the flight attendant to help you or ask other passengers to see if they are willing to switch. If financially possible, upgrade to economy plus for a seat with more room.
- While in your seat, adjust the air vent so that the air blows onto your face. A personal battery operated fan is also good to have with you.
- After arriving at your destination, do what the locals do. If you arrive in the day time, take a walk in the sun even if you are tired. Serotonin, the happy hormone, is produced in the day time and is converted to melatonin at night. Exposure to sunlight helps adjusts your serotonin/melatonin cycle to align with the local rhythm. If you do not align your serotonin/melatonin cycle with the local time, you may suffer from severe jetlag. This may adversely affect your mood. So, remember not only to adjust the time on your watch, but also adjust your biological clock.

- Take vitamin C. The antioxidant will fight fatigue, strengthen the immune system, and lessen stress.
- Do some type of physical activity like walking, running, or working out at a gym.
- Before going to sleep, soak your feet in hot water for twenty minutes. Massage your feet and the San Yin Jiao acupressure point for about two minutes, as described in Chapter 3.

Real Time Diaries

As mentioned in Chapter 3, keeping a detailed diary of your experiences during depression can be useful in discovering ways to battle against the 3-limbed monster. The remaining pages of this chapter contain examples of diary entries I wrote during my depression.

April 21, 2012, Saturday – My first diary entry

For a few nights now, I have not been able to fall asleep peacefully. After thinking about it again and again, I cannot figure out the reason(s) why. Maybe if I list the things I've been thinking about, I can examine them later to help me find the answers I'm looking for.

No. 1: My parents-in-law came at the end of March. They will stay with us briefly. They do the laundry, clean the dishes, and cook for us. They help us and take care of us. Is this making me feel guilty?

No. 2: The company I am consulting for suddenly reduced my time from two days a week to one day a week. I am a little unhappy about this. I contribute a lot to them and feel that I should be doing more work.

No. 3: The lease for the building we do business in expires next year. We are looking for a much bigger place, triple the size of the current place. I feel a little stressed out about it, although this big change should bring us a better financial future.

No. 4: In June, our whole family will visit China. I am worried that I will have a panic attack again, like the one I had in 2001. The kids are all grown up now, so it should be fine this time. More so, I now know what to do to cope, like eat more fruits, drink more water, sleep more, do physical activities, expose myself to sunlight etc. Also this time is different than the last, as the conflict between my parents on buying another apartment has been resolved. I should not be worried at all.

Everything is accounted for. It seems like I am searching for worries. Why? I am not sure. Each time I enter into this state of agitation, everything seems to bother me, even my tooth implant and retainer.

The good news is that my husband is very patient. He listens to me talk and talk. He may not able to understand me, but he keeps on encouraging me while quietly listening to my rambling.

I notice that whenever I can't stay calm at night, I get out of bed, stand in front of the window, and look outside. It's so quiet. The twinkling street lights are not sleeping either.

Neither are the stars in the sky. The street lights and the stars keep me company. I squeeze my hands trying to calm down.

If there is a God, I'd love to believe in you. Please reveal the answers to me. I have always believed in science, but I am willing to trust in God now if doing so helps me calm down and be peaceful and settled. I want to feel grateful for everything I have - family, a husband, children, parents, brothers, sisters, a job, a boss, co-workers, friends, a house, etc.

Today I went to a gathering of old friends including classmates. Several of us walked around the neighborhood and chatted. The main topic was whether people should have stress or not, and what to do about it if you're stressed. We compared life in graduate school with life after, and wondered why we think more now and feel less happy.

In order to overcome the unconformable feelings inside, I am deciding to focus more on myself. Tomorrow, after I drop my kids off at Sunday Chinese school, I will go to the gym. After that, at 11 a.m., I will go to church. I will also call my physician to see if I need to see a psychologist to find out if I should have a full physical exam. I need to find out from the doctor what I should be paying attention to, like food and other things.

Today, the weather was hot. I opened all of the windows at night. Now it is already half past 2 a.m. The intoxicating fragrance coming into the house from the flowers outside smells so good! I am hoping that this pleasant aroma will help me fall asleep.

May 5, 2012, Saturday –
Pep talk to myself to be grateful, strong and confident
Today, I went to my friend's house to learn about detoxification through acupuncture. She showed me several important acupressure points like San Yin Jiao (SP 6), Bai Hui (GV 20) and Yong Quan (KD 1). I don't remember everything she said, but I will give it a try. I Googled the points when I got home and they all came up with pictures and labels!

My sentiment right now is to enjoy what I have. This is such a simple thing, but it has so much meaning. No matter good or bad, like it or not, you accept what God offers you. You have to face life with a peace of mind. Accepting reality will prepare you to enjoy what you have. This reality includes people who may come to live with you. Changes require adjustment. You need to face changes, and enjoy all that you have, because this is what God has offered you. Everything has a reason and meaning. Please don't resist, only embrace. I've decided to do so, and it's not a big deal. The sky is not falling. I should be confident. I can and will accept what God has arranged in my life. Be confident!

May 18, 2012, Friday – Anxiety over travelling to China
I want to feel happy. I am trying to open my mind so that I can be happy. These are the things I am worried about right now:

I am worried about having a panic attack when we fly back to China.

I am worried that my husband will be upset with me for being anxious or having a panic attack.

I am worried about the crowds, noise, and pollution in China.

I am worried that my kids won't be happy, and will complain.

How do I make sure that my kids are happy?

Will exposing myself to of all these worries make me feel better?

May 29, 2012, Tuesday – Hot Flashes
Today I had a hot flash. It happened around 8 a.m. or 9 a.m. this morning during a group meeting. I used a cool wet tissue on the back of my neck to cool myself down. It's amazing how much heat I generate. The cool wet tissue on the back of my neck became hot. I drank a cup of soybean milk in the morning and evening. Soybean milk is said to boost estrogen levels. I hope drinking soy milk can help ease my hot flashes.

March 18, 2013, Monday – Sadness brought on by the gap between dreams and reality
Sometimes, sadness and emptiness come over my mind like a tidal wave. The change is sudden and unaccountable. My sadness condenses into tear drops. I want to cry, but do not know what to cry for. Perhaps for the inevitability of aging, the irreversible signs of growing older, fading estrogen, and the loss of all the joy, happiness, longing, and excitement associated with being young.

Why do I feel bothered when there is nothing to bother me? Is it because of the gap between my dreams and the reality of my life? When I was young, I dreamed of having great relationships, achievements, and happiness. That future, dreamt long ago, is now. If 'youth is the smile of the future in the presence of an unknown quantity, which is itself', said by Hugo,[16] then growing old is a reality check. I can do so little. I can't make a difference. I know so little. My capability is so limited. I have no way of filling in the gap between my dreams and my reality. The gap is getting wider as I become older. I do not feel needed and fear that I will eventually become a burden to my kids, to my husband, and to the society. I am moving toward a state of not being valuable - to nothingness.

Is this the cause of my sadness? How do I fix it? Everyone is the same. There are no exceptions. I am just one of many. Let the tears flow, they are the flow of true feelings. The young are full of life. They are busy hoping for, dreaming about, and preparing for a wonderful future. I prepared myself for life in all aspects. The journey becomes a lasting memory. After we die, our lives continue in another form, but the basic elements will forever be the same.

In the meantime, how do we keep negativity in check? I think that keeping your brain healthy is the most important thing. We need to talk to people and train ourselves to be logical. We need to do things that cheer us up, even if it's for a few seconds.

March 5, 2014, Tuesday –
Panic attack after recovering from depression
I had been fine for a while, but yesterday it happened again. Now I need to write down what happened. I ate a lot for dinner - two pieces of Chinese pizza, half a plate of stir fried rice, no vegetables. I was very tired, as I had been working in front

of the computer reviewing files all day. After dinner, I lied down on the sofa and slept for about an hour.

Around 10:30 pm, I cleaned up and went to bed. I wanted to finish reading a book, but could not resist the TV. I wanted to watch the news about the Russian invasion of the Ukraine. After that, I watched Forensic Files and CNN until 12 a.m. One of the stories on TV got my mind working. This made me feel a little panicked, so I turned off the TV. After turning the TV off, I still felt anxious, excited, and numb. Why did I feel numb? My brain wondered off. I could not control and was not able to know where it was going. In the end, I got stuck at a point where there was no resolution. I tossed and turned. I tried to reading my book and watching TV, but neither took my mind out of that state. I could not stay still in bed. What did I do afterwards? I meditated for 15 minutes, did 20 squats, 10 sit-ups, drank four or five cups of water, mopped the floor, and hand washed some clothing that had been waiting to be washed for quite a while. Afterwards, I stood in the stairway to look outside, then walked back and forth in the hallway. The only thing I could do to keep my mind from wandering was to move around.

At last, at about 2 a.m., I felt better. I went back to bed and gradually drifted back to sleep. I did not wake up again until my alarm went off. This was my second successful experience conquering a panic attack and insomnia with intense physical activity. The physical activities put me back in control.

March 15, 2015, Sunday – Thoughts on panic attacks
The mind works differently when in a state of anxiety. It seems like the area controlling the positive aspect of the mind is

dormant. Negative thoughts dominate. If I put it in a scenario of light and dark, dark beats out the light in panic attack mode. The light is nowhere to be found. I am incapable of putting in the effort to go back into the light. The dark force is so strong. The dark represents regret, fear and guilt - events and experiences from the past that I wish to undo come back and torture me. I feel like there's no way out and no resolution as these memories are permanent and irreversible. The list of memories that trigger these flashbacks seems endless - just one word or sight can bring them forward. Why is it that only negative thoughts dominate, overwhelm, and control me? Why should my mind work differently now? The negative memories have always been there, inactive, and under control. Why have I lost control now?

The brain, where the mind resides, is supposed to block out all kinds of undesirable things. Does the condition of the brain and environment have something to do with losing control of the mind? What impacts the workings of the brain? Is it ion balance, oxygen, nutrients, blood, food, rest, exhaustion, over use, drugs or alcohol? What is it that influences my brain in this state of anxiety chemically, physically, or biologically? I've noticed that my anxiety happens more often at night. Thoughts of having no way out, that what is done cannot be undone, coupled with the fear of the future, all seem to be magnified by the darkness. Why is my imagination overcome with negativity?

When a panic attack begins, it makes me jump - the sense of losing control takes me over and I started behaving crazy. I want to escape. I stomp my feet, frown, walk back and forth, and want to get out from wherever I am. I want to eliminate all of the things that bother me in that instant to relieve the panic and ease my mind. When my mind and body are in chaos, I am not me. Physical suffering manifests in pain. Mental suffering manifests in chaos of the conscience.

When in a state of panic, I often think about the statement, "one day, she became crazy." I recalled hearing this when I was young - when a person in my village went crazy. My mother said that the person was visited by a ghost. Hearing this made me afraid that ghosts visited everyone. My mother tried to reassure me that they didn't visit everyone. They only visited the weak. I wondered what kind people were weak, and if I were one of them. My mother replied that sickly looking people were weak. I then wondered how sickly people looked. My mother replied that sickly people look like the woman who went crazy. She always looked as through the wind could blow her away. If you are physically strong, your face should be pink or red. Your muscles should look strong when you are active, and the ghosts will be afraid of you and will stay away. My mother told me not to be lazy. She told me to be active in strengthening my body so that I wouldn't have to worry about ghosts.

Oct 1, 2017, Sunday – Understanding panic attacks through documented experience

I had a panic attack today. After breakfast, I drove to the salon for my once a month facial. After my facial I went to a spa to have a massage. That's when my panic attack occurred. While being lead into the room, I started to worry about the size of the room. Maybe it would be too small, like the room I had a panic attack in before. However, the room I was led into ended up being a spacious room with a window. I felt lucky and relieved. As I got undressed, I started to feel annoyed. Maybe the light was too dim, making me feel dizzy. I opened the curtain to let the light in and then felt fine again. I lied down and my attention landed on the music. It was the same music that the spa had always played. It had never bothered me before, but was bothering me now. The masseuse came in and I asked her if she could turn the music down. She said that it was centrally controlled so she could not change it. This made me feel really bothered. I started to feel that the room was hot, stuffy, and noisy. The hair sticking to my neck was irritating me. The masseuse was very patient and kind. She tied my hair back and allowed me to lie with my head turned sideways instead of facing down. She started to massage my neck, head and shoulders. My mind started to wander into negative thoughts, just like before. I wanted to leave the room, but forced myself to stay. I told myself that it would pass. I pinched my leg hard to distract my mind, but my leg felt like rubber. It was no use. I tried to focus my mind on the massage, but I could not. I remember thinking that sixty minutes was too long! I could not be still there for sixty minutes. With the intention to avert my mind, I started a casual conversation with the masseuse. After about ten minutes, I started to calm down. About half way through, I became fine. I found that starting a conversation with her seemed to avert a full on panic attack! Little by little, as the conversation continued, my pleasure sensations returned, and I was able to enjoy the rest of the massage.

On my way back home, I told myself to write the experience down as one more n=1 data point. I realized that the last time I had a panic attack was two years ago. That time I had Chinese buffet for lunch. This time, I had Chinese food the night before - interesting.

I think that this panic attack may have come on because of feelings I had about my daughter leaving home for college. The empty nest made me feel down and empty. Yesterday, I spent five to six hours volunteering and listening to seminars on artificial intelligence. Afterward, I did not go back to my empty house. I decided to go to my favorite Chinese restaurant for dinner instead. I ordered eggplant over noodles in a clay pot, which was very savory. I also had a red bean smoothie, which was very sweet. I typically order tea as the drink, but did not last night. After that, I went home and talked to my daughter on the phone until 1 am. This morning, we ate the leftover noodles. Everything seemed fine in the morning, but my empty nest has been getting me down. I have been crying a lot recently. Music and stories, happy or sad, make me cry. This could be a sign of my weakening mental state.

Just prior to a panic attack, I tend to worry more about peoples' attitudes towards me. For example, before my massage, I went to a clothing store to kill some time. There was a guy standing at the door greeting everyone who entered. I did not hear him greet me and the cashier did not say hello to me when it was checking out. This bothered me. When I got to the spa, I went to the bathroom. Less than one minute later, I heard a knock at the door. The lady who knocked saw me go in, so I was annoyed that she was knocking on the door. What was the hurry? These sensitivities might have been signs that a panic attack was mounting. When these types of things happen with people, I can usually brush them off. Maybe the staff at the clothing store saw my intense face and did not dare to say hello. Who knows?

The night before my panic attack, I had a good night's sleep.

So lack of sleep did not contribute to my anxiety. I checked my diary and noticed that the last time I had a panic attack, it happened after eating Chinese food. Is this a coincidence? Is Monosodium glutamate (MSG) the problem? I Googled "MSG" and read about the side effects. Per Wikipedia, MSG is a popular food additive that improves taste. Glutamates are important neurotransmitters in the human brain. I then googled "MSG and panic attacks". Sure enough, I found what I was looking for. My intuition was right. I was not alone. People shared stories about having panic attacks after eating Chinese food. This does not happen in all people, but for some, MSG has caused panic attacks. Others state that MSG bothers the stomach. Both reactions happened to me. My mind itself was already in a shaky state, and so consuming MSG may have been the last straw in triggering my panic attack. Having a panic attack after consuming MSG is my n=2 data point. I eat Chinese food all the time, but rarely have panic attacks. To validate the cause and effect relationship, I need more data points.

It is all about actions! Keeping diaries or activity logs provides clues for finding internal or external reasons that may be throwing off your yin-yang balance. The world is balanced with Yin and Yang, night and day, high and low. It is everything. We strive to keep our "fight-or-flight" and "rest-and-digest" cycle as natural and smooth as possible, so that we can achieve a peaceful mind and a happy life. Intense, physical activity is critical to achieving this balance. Discovering these tips and tricks inspired me to draw a remedy pie chart of my own, consisting of three slices; 10% realizing you are depressed, and deciding to act instead of dwell on the misery, 30% self-analysis, and 60% action. Just do it!

CHAPTER 5

Maintenance and Beyond

Movement

ALBERT EINSTEIN SAID that "Life is like riding a bicycle: to keep your balance you must keep moving." Life relies on motion. However, compared with our ancient ancestors, we are less physically active. This is due to human innovation. All innovations stem from human laziness since they provide convenience, comfort, and instant gratification. Life is so much easier now than it was for our ancestors – we drive everywhere and have machines for heavy lifting, fruit picking, crop harvesting, and feeding animals. Being physically fit is no longer a requirement for survival. We don't need muscular men to hunt for our food. We don't need women to be hyper-feminine to attract men for the sake of reproduction. Nearly everyone born into modern civilization can survive with little need to re-define or re-enforce the strongest. On the highway, a petite five-foot tall woman can go just as fast on the highway as the muscular six-foot tall man driving next to her.

With modern life being so comparatively easy, why do we

experience so much anxiety and panic? It may be due to the lack of movement we now have in our daily lives. Historically, humans hunted and labored for survival. They did not sit still for hours or days working on computers, watching TV, or playing video games. Perhaps the anxiety we experience is our body's way of telling us that something is abnormal. Being sedentary has not been part of our evolutionary development until now. Our bodies and brains are not wired for it. When you overwork your muscles, your muscles ache. When you overwork your eyes, your eyes get sore. When you overwork your mind, your mental state diminishes. Any activity done in excess can throw the body and the mind off balance.

The purpose of daily physical activity is to maintain a balance between your physical and mental state. Physical activity may eliminate the chemicals associated with the fight-or-flight stress responses built up throughout the day. It speeds up the circulation of blood which carries necessary nutrients to the brain and removes waste.

Whenever possible, I choose to maximize opportunities for physical activity on a daily basis. The effort may seem insignificant at first, but when the habit of choosing physical activity is formed, the benefits add up and make a difference. I often take short walks with co-workers after lunch and climb the stairs to my 6th floor office. Instead of making a phone call or writing an email to a co-worker, I walk to their desk. According to a paper published by Levine JA on non-exercise activity thermogenesis (NEAT),[17] even trivial physical activities increase metabolic rate substantially and have a cumulative impact. NEAT could be a critical component in maintaining our body weight. NEAT is the energy expended for everything we do that is not sleeping, eating or exercising. It Includes the energy expended from walking to work, typing, performing yard work, undertaking agricultural tasks and fidgeting. I believe that these minor physical activities may mimic the busy daily work of our ancestors. With all of this in mind, I often say to myself, "Don't be lazy. Move!"

In addition to being conscious of my NEAT levels, whenever I feel any numbing of the mind before bed, I do at least thirty squats. As I mentioned before, doing squats always enables me to breathe deeply. Every other day, after showering, I do thirty eight sit-ups. Afterwards, I lie on top of my bed and focus on deep breathing. This makes me feel content and energized. Soaking my feet in hot water, and foot massages helps keep me relax and sleep.

Diet and Sleep

Among all of my organs, my stomach is particularly sensitive to stress and anxiety. Although it can be difficult to have a well-balanced diet and stay hydrated during anxiety and depression, it is key to ensuring that the body is supplied with nutrients and anti-oxidants to quench the free radicals generated through bioprocesses. Free radicals are high-energy molecules with unpaired electrons. These high-energy molecules look for other molecules to pair up with and can be quite destructive. Antioxidants, like Vitamin C, can stop this process by quenching free radicals. Vitamin C should be taken with its food source for maximum antioxidant benefit.

Eating regularly without overeating yourself is important. Before eating, be sure to reduce any anxiety or stress as much as possible to ensure proper digestion. After eating, be sure to wait about twenty minutes before exercising for the same reason. Massaging acupressure points related to the stomach may also help increase the appetite and aid in digestion by stimulating its functionality.

Getting enough sleep is critical for maintaining a healthy mental state. Do your best to expose yourself to the sunlight during the day to aid in falling asleep at night. Relax and allow the brain to rest and complete its self-maintenance.

Dealing with Negativity

Negative emotions can result from a myriad of reasons; energy depletion, hormone changes, diminishing vitality, insecurities about status in society, our kids being bullied, the toilet not flushing, the garbage being full, a leaky roof, traffic, the neighbor's dog barking, the smell of the neighbor's cooking, less capable co-workers getting promoted when you believe you are more capable, the cashier not smiling at you when he smiled at the person before you, the waiter not leading you to a good table, nasty YouTube comments, politics, and the news; the list goes on and on.

Unfairness, inconvenience, and hassles exist everywhere and at all times. In our day to day lives, our mood is largely affected by the things happening around us. We may also be impacted by circumstances larger than ourselves. For example, we may oppose the direction that the world is going in and feel like we can't do anything but shout into thin air. Finding excuses can relieve us in the short run. In the long run, it is up to us to remove our own negativity from its root. Feeling malicious, angry, or resentful serves no benefit to ourselves or others. The wheels of human history roll on regardless, so we may as well do our best to remain positive, despite the challenges that we face.

When negative thoughts start creeping into your mind, try to do something to avoid them. Quick activities may help. Try to dance, stretch your legs or arms, take a brisk walk, imitate singing birds, or just sing. For me singing is the best way to escape from negative thoughts. People often sing or hum when they're happy. So singing in a state of stress may also help return our mind to a more positive state. Trying to remember a song's words and tune distracts the mind. Reading can also be a good distraction for the mind to help in escaping negative thoughts. Fighting off negative thoughts may be easier for some than others, but the effort is worth it. For me being grateful helps me feel lucky, happy, patient, forgiving and more understanding.

Perspective on Panic Attacks

Balance in our diet, activities, work, and sleep are key to a healthy mental state. When our bodies are well-rested, they buffer well, and we can handle the small fluctuations. However, when we are on the edge, any little change can push us off the cliff and send us into a state of panic.

Balance requires discipline. It is useful to keep a diary of three categories: what you eat, what you do, and how much you sleep. Keep notes on these three things after you have a panic attack, and work to discover remedies by reading books, searching online, and learning from others' experiences.

There is so much you can do to help yourself. By helping yourself, you build a soft invisible shield against your anxiety and depression. Be your own guinea pig. Don't cry when you have a panic attack. When it happens, smile instead. Maybe you can learn something from it which keeps you from having another one.

Family and Friends of the Depressed

Family and friends play a vital role in most peoples' daily lives. The way our loved ones respond to our anxiety or depression can either help or hinder progress towards recovery. For family and friends of the depressed, lend your ear, and be encouraging - go with the flow and allow the suffering out. People suffering from anxiety or depression are not pretending. They need acceptance and should not be expected to simply snap out of it. No one wants to behave bizarrely or act like a maniac. At one point during my depression, I thought that my dental implant was not mine and wanted to take it out. I thought about my dentist using the word "permanent" when referring to the implant, and the whole idea of it really started to bother me. When I told my husband how I was feeling, he frowned, making me feel even worse. He then suggested that we go back to the dentist and have her remove it. His suggestion made me feel like he was on my side which helped calm me down.

I eventually got over the anxiety involving my implant, and after doing so, I shrugged it off as a moment of being unreasonable. I even laugh at myself whenever I think about it. However, the experience taught me to allow those thoughts from my anxiety and depression to flow instead of trying to stop them with reasoning or logic. In those moments, un-reasonable requests should not be taken literally, but they should also not be blocked or re-directed. Nobody can stop or change the flow of a roaring flood.

Our view of the world is influenced by our mental state. If you are mean, people surrounding you seem mean. If you are nice, people surrounding you seem nice. A depressed person's mind is haunted with paranoia and anxiety and is sometimes incapable of perceiving reality. Their mental state keeps them from being themselves. If you are the family member or friend of a person suffering from depression, say something, and seek help for them. A true loved one or friend would not leave someone to deal with the misery of depression alone. Friendship, love and society's safety net, when summoned to-gether, can be powerful forces in the fight against depression.

Questions from Chapter 2 - Answered

In Chapter 2, you may recall a list of some questions I asked myself during my depression. Although my suffering was not completely eliminated through self-study and learning from experience, I gained confidence in aswering some of the questions I had early on about my depression.

1) I don't have anything to complain about in my life. Why am I so depressed?

Depression has little to do with external factors. I be-lieve that it is mostly due to our physiology. Thinking back on my life as it was before my depression, I re-member cruising along with a clear conscious and being totally in control. However, at the onset of age-related hormone changes, I became depressed. This is a natural process that may last several years before menopause begins. Estrogen, testosterone and progesterone spike and fall irregularly during pre-menopause and menopause. These hormones impact our mood, health and behavior. Estrogen is believed to affect the production of serotonin, the neurotrans-mitter associated with happiness. Fluctuating levels of estrogen, may impact the levels of serotonin, or happy chemicals, in the body. For some, the fluctuat-ing levels of hormones and neurotransmitters result in a stronger response, while others may have no response, and still others may have an intermediate response. It is also interesting to know that sex hor-mones and stress-induced cortisol are all produced from the same starting material, cholesterol via their own enzymatic biosynthesis process in the body. I guess the amount and timing of the production of a certain enzyme causing the reaction to occur varies from person to person. It is said that women may ex-perience severe mood swings either at puberty or pre-menopause, but seldom at both. In either case, once hormone levels even out life returns to normal.

2) Each woman goes through menopause and not all of them go through depression. What is so unique about me? Where does my tendency to be attacked by the 3-limbed monster come from?

Menopause is different for everyone. The average age for the onset of menopause is fifty one. However, the time of onset and magnitude of a women's response to the changes in hormone levels is different from person to person. For women who have given birth to more kids and have breastfed, the onset of pre-menopause or menopause is delayed. Menopause begins when a woman's last egg is released, and the number of eggs a woman has varies. The delay in menopause due to having children may be as much as nine months for each birth, plus the months of breastfeeding after giving birth.

The physiological changes, in combination with each woman's unique personality and emotional characteristics, may explain the variety in women's responses to pre-menopause and menopause. Our personalities and emotional characteristics are as unique as finger prints. I naturally tend to be sensitive, fearful and often irritable, as a result of my strong fight-or-flight response. This makes me more vulnerable to extreme emotions, such as anxiety and depression. I believe that my body's natural hormonal changes, coupled with my tendency to be highly alert and responsive, made me twice as vulnerable to anxiety and depression during pre-menopause and menopause.

3)   Am I mentally ill? If so, why now?

I was not mentally ill. If I were mentally ill, I would have known a long time before the onset of pre-menopause.

I had been fine my whole life until my sudden depression at the onset of pre-menopause. The fluctuations in my hormone levels pushed my mood and sanity off a cliff. With the passing of menopause, my life returned to normal, minus the flirty reactions towards men associated with my youth. I am now more settled in myself and am happier.

4) Am I ever going to recover? Is this misery going to end?

Absolutely! In times of struggle, I was a little tiny boat engulfed by a tempest in a dark, vast, angry sea. Although terrifying, every storm ends – and each ending is usually met with a beautiful day.

5) Is taking antidepressants going to be my only option for fighting the 3-limbed monster?

Of course not! Finding ways to reduce stress naturally may be the best medicine of all. Do whatever you can to reduce those triggers which may increase your vulnerability to depression. The stress response cycle is like fighting off a tiger, and can be completed by physical activity. Doing squats, soaking my feet in hot water, and practicing acupressure were the most effective activities for me in my fight against anxiety and depression. Use yourself as a guinea pig to find out what works for you. Antidepressants, such as fluoxetine "Prozac", or sertraline "Zoloft", mimic natural neurotransmitters like serotonin. The side effects are proven to be acceptable, and are safe if used carefully under a doctor's supervision. Although I did not have to use antidepressants to fight off my three-limbed monster, it gave me comfort in knowing that they were available as a last resort. People in modern times are fortunate to have antidepressants to help in the fight against depression.

6) I have known people who have committed suicide. Will I suffer the same fate?

No. Suicide is the coldest word. In the Chinese culture, the word is quite taboo; we can only whisper it as it is an unnatural phenomenon. Most people suffering from depression do not want to burden those whom they love with their problems, but committing suicide hurts the people they leave behind for the rest of their lives. The livings are tortured with the guilt of not being able to help. There should be only one option for those suffering from depression - to fight and win. Get help from a professional. Look inside and outside yourself. Have faith in yourself and your doctor. Realize that there are so many doors to walk through and people with caring hearts. The Bible says "Ask, and it shall be given you; seek, and ye shall find; knock, and it shall be opened unto you" - no matter how faint the sound of your knocking is. Keep in mind that, as you move along in life, periods of great difficulty are transitional. Difficult times eventually become faint memories. As it is said in Victor Hugo's Les Misérables, "Even the darkest night will end and the sun will rise."

7) If each experience has its own meaning, what is the meaning of this depression for me?

The meaning of each person's experience is for them to define. For me, learning how to cope with my depression, and being able to share my experiences with others in hopes that they can help is very meaningful. I made a promise to myself to take my depression and turn it into something positive to share with the world. In a sense, I have defined my meaning as helping other suffering souls.

8) What is the purpose for me living on anyway?

Albert Einstein wrote:

Our situation on this earth seems strange. Every one of us appears here, involuntarily and uninvited, for a short stay, without knowing the why and the wherefore. In our daily lives we feel only that man is here for the sake of others, for those whom we love and for many other beings whose fate is connected with our own.

I often hike a popular trail near my home called the Golden Eagle trail. The trail is long, and rolls smoothly through the hills. From the hill tops, you can see the entire valley, with a bird's eye view of highways, houses, and shopping centers. From high up on the hill top, all of these things seem to be in harmony.

At age fifty I feel that I have made it to the hill top of life. Far removed in space and time from my early life, I can begin to look back on all of my busy years of climbing. I am now settled and free to enjoy the essence of life. The role I value most in life is being a mother, then a daughter, then a wife, then a useful member of society. I have a loving and supporting cast around me; my parents, my family, and my friends. It is my duty to not just live on for myself, but for those around me who I value so much.

While struggling with my 3-limbed monster, my quest for happiness suddenly became my main focus. During that time, I questioned the purpose of my life very often. At one point, I realized that instead of searching for some grand answer for the meaning of life, I could decide life's meaning for myself. Instead of asking "why am I here", and "what is my purpose for living", I starting saying "since I am here, what can I make out of this life, and how do I define my own significance?"

For me, the purpose of life is to be happy and make a positive contribution to the world, whether it's by being a great mother, daughter, wife, or member of society. This requires much effort, both mentally and physically, but being a positive force in the world, with sustained happiness as a goal, is worthwhile. For me focusing on feeling blessed helps lighten my heart and clear my spirit. When I start feeling down, I cheer myself up by purposefully counting my blessings. Only when we are happy can we accomplish the important work of making others happy, and bringing the positive energy into the world.

When our lives on Earth are over, our bodies become dust. This dust is composed of basic chemical elements which never disappear. These elements become the building blocks for new living things. Our genes may pass on to the next generation, and I believe that our souls join an invisible cloud of human souls. In this sense, life becomes eternal. In the end, as written by Albert Einstein, "Everything is determined, the beginning as well as the end, by forces over which we have no control. It is determined for the insect, as well as for the star. Human beings, vegetables, or cosmic dust, we all dance to a mysterious tune, intoned in the distance by an invisible piper."

With this in mind, it is important that we make the most of our time here on Earth. Given our unique circumstances, we should try to leave a lasting and positive impact on the world around us, so that when everything is over, not only will our genes be passed on to the next generation, but our personal stories as well. Our individual struggles only exist so that we may fight through them, and our inevitable victories will be our legacy.

Acknowledgements

I would like to thank my friends for sharing all their tips on dealing with depression.

I would also like to thank those who contribute on Wikipedia. Without your knowledge and discoveries, I would not have become enlightened.

I would like to thank you for all your anonymous internet posts on sharing your experience and struggles and giving me the comfort of not being alone. I want to hear your stories as well as share mine and be able to pass them on to others.

I would like to thank my parents and siblings for their guidance as well as their confidence and expectations of me to become better.

I would like to thank my editor and co-author, Tiffany J. Towsley. Thank you for joining me on this project. Without you, I would not be able to complete this work.

Lastly, I would like to thank my family, for putting up with me during those struggling times as well as all your help on this book. I feel blessed to share my life with you.

Notes

1   American Psychiatric Association. (Jan 2017). What Is
     Depression?. Retrieved from https://www.psychiatry.org/
     patients-families/depression/what-is-depression

2   Anxiety and Depression Association of America.
     Symptoms. Retrieved from https://adaa.org/un-
     derstanding-anxiety/panic-disorder-agoraphobia/
     symptoms#

3   Diagnostic and Statistical Manual of Mental
     DisordersAmerican Psychiatric Associati (5th ed.).
     Arlington: American Psychiatric Publishing. 2013. pp.
     189–195. ISBN 978-0890425558.

4   Mezzacappa E, Katkin E, Palmer S (1999). "Epinephrine,
     arousal, and emotion: A new look at two-factor
     theory". Cognition and Emotion. 13 (2): 181–199.
     doi:10.1080/026999399379320

5   Toth M, Ziegler M, Sun P, Gresack J, Risbrough V
     (February 2013). "Impaired conditioned fear response
     and startle reactivity in epinephrine-deficient mice".

Behavioural Pharmacology. 24 (1): 1–9. doi:10.1097/FBP.0b013e32835cf408. PMC 3558035 . PMID 23268986

6   The Metamorphosis and Other Stories by Franx Kafka

7   Richard Wright, Black Boy (New York, HarperCollins, 2005), 119

8   Harvard Medical School, "Understanding the Stress Response – Chronic Activation of this Survival Mechanism Impairs health," Published, March 2011, Updated, March 18, 2016, https://www.health.harvard.edu/staying-healthy/understanding-the-stress-response

9   "Dopamine". PubChem. Retrieved 21 September 2015.

10 Yamashima T (May 2003). "Jokichi Takamine (1854-1922), the samurai chemist, and his work on adrenalin". Journal of Medical Biography. 11 (2): 95–102. PMID 12717538

11 Scott E (2011-09-22). "Cortisol and Stress: How to Stay Healthy". About.com. Retrieved 2011-11-29

12 Colette Bouchez, "Serotonin: 9 Questions and Answers," October 12, 2011, https://www.webmd.com/depression/features/serotonin#1

13 González-Flores D, Velardo B, Garrido M, González-Gómez D, Lozano M, Ayuso M.C, Barriga C, Paredes S.D, Rodríguez A.B. (2011). "Ingestion of Japanese plums

(Prunus salicina Lindl. cv. Crimson Globe) increases the urinary 6-sulfatoxymelatonin and total antioxidant capacity levels in young, middle-aged and elderly humans: Nutritional and functional characterization of their content". Journal of Food and Nutrition Research. 50 (4): 229–236.

14 Evsikov A, 2008, Weerasinghe D, 2013, MetaCyc Pathway: serotonin and melatonin biosynthesis

15 Integrative Psychiatry.Hormone Balance. Retrieved from https://www.integrativepsychiatry.net/hormone_balance

16 Victor Hugo, Les Meserables (Gutenberg, EBook #135, June 22, 2008), http://www.gutenberg.org/files/135/135-h/135-h

17 Levine JA, "Non-exercise activity thermogenesis (NEAT)," Best Pract Res Clin Endocrinol Metab. 2002 Dec;16(4):679-702, https://www.ncbi.nlm.nih.gov/pubmed/12468415

CPSIA information can be obtained
at www.ICGtesting.com
Printed in the USA
BVHW04s2228190518
516621BV00005B/204/P

9 781478 796619